JULIE LE CLERC

SIMPLE DELI FOOD

PHOTOGRAPHY
SHAUN CATO-SYMONDS

PENGUIN BOOKS

This book is for those who may wish to discover something more exotic but don't know where to start. It is for those who want to extend their culinary repertoire. And it is for those who love tasty, spirited cooking and are constantly seeking new combinations. I have created these flavour-orientated recipes with sometimes familiar and other times more unusual deli-style ingredients. Use them as guides to increase your knowledge and experience of such ingredients and as a springboard for your own creativity. They exist for the pure joy of making something delicious to eat.

'Delicatessen' originates from a word meaning delicacies, so I'm not talking about downright weird things. I'm simply referring to delicious foodstuffs that range from quality breads, chocolate and engaging flavourings to staples such as good pasta and rice. The aim here is not to replicate these items but to incorporate them into dishes. In other words, this book is about how to use, say, bread or pesto as ingredients, rather than how to actually make bread or pesto. Having said this, there are a few exceptions, such as my secret recipe for continental deli-style sticky sugar buns.

We are fortunate to have access to an increasing selection of fantastic ingredients and a wide choice of places to procure them. The Larousse Gastronomique cookery encyclopaedia describes delicatessen as 'a shop selling high-quality groceries and luxury food products'. Contemporary shops of this ilk range from traditional European-style delicatessens, speciality food stores, swelling supermarket deli-sections and ethnic food markets. The latter may not be called deli by name but definitely are delicatessens by nature. For example, Indian food emporiums, Asian supermarkets or Middle Eastern grocers are veritable treasure chests full of flavours to be explored.

Think of delicatessens as giant store cupboards holding a wealth of inspiration and flavour options. While every cook's pantry needs a stock of essentials, my advice is to also shop for interesting, quality ingredients that will add sparkle to your cooking. For example, seasonings such as potent sauces and exotic spices are vibrant elements that will enliven simple dishes. These concentrated ingredients can be transported home and utilised to enhance fresh produce and achieve food of exceptional flavour; food cooked with ease and pleasure.

When I sat down to compose a list of deli ingredients to work with, my inventory grew way beyond the pages of this book. I knew it would be impossible to cover all of these ingredients in one small volume. I have therefore limited my selection to the most interesting and least obscure, while at the same time striving to present some new challenges and inspiration. Where possible, I have endeavoured to give several recipe options for each ingredient featured.

You may note that I have only touched on the vast and varied flavours of the Asian pantry. More and more European-style delis now display stocks of Asian ingredients because our eating habits have embraced them. This is not fusion, which I think can cause confusion, but relates very definitely to an increased demand for these alluring flavours. I have included some such ingredients in this book where appropriate. However, I feel there are many notable books by authors I respect that cover these specialist ingredients in greater depth than I could ever attempt to in this particular book.

I hope that *Simple Deli Food* may begin to demystify the wonderful profusion of delicatessen ingredients available. While this is not a definitive guide, there is a glossary at the end of each chapter to help identify and explain the ingredients featured in this book. I have given substitutions where possible for those who may live in places lacking a variety of specialised food stores. To gain confidence with new flavours, aim to regularly combine common foods already on hand with newfound elements. I feel sure that once introduced to these ingredients, and with a bit of experimentation and practice, you will feel very comfortable using them and they will become familiar allies in the kitchen.

When it's all boiled down, this book is about recipes – simple recipes for making something delicious to eat. It is about building an understanding of distinctive ingredients and incorporating them into everyday cooking. It is also firmly about flavour. These recipes demonstrate how increased knowledge and use of interesting ingredients can add intoxicating flavour to food and transform simple dishes into taste sensations.

ACKNOWLEDGEMENTS

I wish to extend my heartfelt thanks to those who have supported me in this project. I consider myself very fortunate to work with people I hugely respect and admire. I am honoured by your friendships. Special thanks go to:

Shaun Cato-Symonds, photographer – for working with me to create these glorious food pictures of enduring quality and beauty.
Katrina Tanner, model – for gracing the pages of this book with your lovely presence and for your valued friendship.
Bernice Beachman, Penguin Books (NZ), publisher – for having such faith in my work and for your warm spirit and extraordinary insight.
Philippa Gerrard, Penguin editor – for your enthusiastic support and encouragement and gentle editing skills that have allowed me to find my own voice.
Athena Sommerfeld, designer – I owe you a debt of gratitude for the rare beauty of this book's arrangement and for its user-friendly feel.
Thanks to Shelley Gare, editor of *Sunday Life,* Australia, for my exciting new Australian connection.
And thank you to all the numerous and willing eaters who form my trusted tasting panel and provide feedback during the recipe testing process.

Grateful thanks go to these delicatessens and specialised food stores for existing to provide exceptional products, advice and dedicated friendly service:
Kapiti Cheeses, Auckland – for offering a most astounding selection of delicious international cheeses. Special thanks to Cory Morgan, photographed holding the magnificent wheel of cheese, and Rachel Everett for your generous assistance.
Mahadeo's, Auckland – a specialist spice house and suppliers of a fascinating array of grains and pulses; thanks for allowing us to photograph in-store.
Moore Wilson's Fresh, Wellington – for providing exciting comestibles and such a remarkable food shopping experience. Thanks for your support and advice.
Sabato, Auckland – for the inspiration I always gain from your exquisite imported food products and for your uncompromising commitment to quality.
Zarbo Delicatessen, Auckland – for allowing us to photograph many of the atmospheric black and white shots portraying deli ingredients used in this book. And for searching to offer such a comprehensive and extraordinary range of foodstuffs.

Many thanks to these stores for providing beautiful tableware as props for food styling and photography: Country Road Homeware, Freedom Furniture, Nest.

CONTENTS

THIS CHAPTER IS NOT SO MUCH ABOUT HOW TO REPLICATE SPECIALITY BREADS FOUND IN THE DELI BUT MORE ABOUT HOW TO USE BREAD AS A BASIC INGREDIENT IN MANY DIFFERENT KINDS OF DISHES, FROM SANDWICHES TO BREAD PUDDING. SOME RECIPES ARE FOR BREAD DERIVATIVES; THESE INCLUDE CROSTINI AND BRUSCHETTA. OTHERS ARE FOR PERFECT ACCOMPANIMENTS TO BREAD SUCH AS SPREADS AND PRESERVES. THERE ARE AS MANY RECIPE POSSIBILITIES FOR USING LEFTOVER BREAD AS THERE ARE STYLES OF BREAD AVAILABLE. SOME RECIPES TELL THE SECRETS OF HOW TO MAKE CERTAIN SPECIALITY BREADS AND BAKED GOODS THAT ARE TYPICALLY FOUND IN EUROPEAN-STYLE DELICATESSENS.

BRUSCHETTA WITH PEA & MINT SPREAD

Bruschetta can be thought of as an exotic form of toast, fragrant with garlic and anointed with olive oil. Bruschetta is the perfect base for any topping, from pesto such as this pea spread, to simplicity itself — crushed fresh tomatoes.

sliced sourdough, ciabatta or other
rustic bread
4 cloves garlic, peeled and cut in half
extra virgin olive oil

1 To make the bruschetta, chargrill or toast the bread on both sides. Rub garlic into one side and drizzle with extra virgin olive oil.

PEA AND MINT SPREAD

1 cup peas (frozen or blanched fresh)
1 clove garlic, peeled
2 tblsp chopped fresh mint
2 tblsp freshly grated Parmesan
juice of 1 lemon
2 tblsp extra virgin olive oil
salt and freshly ground black pepper

1 Pound peas and garlic in a mortar and pestle or pulse in a food processor until thick but still textural.
2 Stir in mint, Parmesan, lemon juice and oil and season to taste with salt and pepper.
3 Spread on hot bruschetta to serve.

MAKES 1½ CUPS

THE BEST HAM AND CHEESE SANDWICH

This is not difficult, of course, but it is one of the best-ever sandwich combinations. A perfect result relies totally upon the quality of the ingredients — the bread, ham and cheese must all be top-notch.

8 slices quality bread of choice
8 slices quality ham off the bone
8 slices flavoursome cheese such as
Gruyère, Jarlsberg, Manchego or an
aged Cheddar

1 Top 4 slices bread with generous amounts of ham and cheese. Top with remaining slices of bread.
2 If the bread, ham and cheese are all fresh and with excellent flavour then nothing more is needed, not even butter in my opinion. This is not to say that butter, chutney or anything else you fancy can't be included if desired. Toasting the sandwich is another option that will totally change the sandwich's consistency.

MAKES 4

NEW YORK RUBEN ON RYE

A Ruben is a classic sandwich that features in every self-respecting New York delicatessen.

8 slices rye bread

Dijon mustard

8 slices corned beef

8 slices Gruyère cheese

I cup sauerkraut (finely sliced,
  fermented cabbage available in
  cans from the deli)

1/2 red pepper, roasted, seeds removed

1/4 cup basic mayonnaise (see page 101)

salt and freshly ground black pepper

1   Spread 4 slices bread with mustard. Layer 2 slices of corned beef and 2 slices Gruyère cheese on each and top with a good spoonful of drained sauerkraut.

2   Purée roasted red pepper into prepared mayonnaise. Spoon dressing on top of sauerkraut, sprinkle with salt and pepper to taste. Top with remaining slices of bread.

MAKES 4

PANZANELLA

Intriguing, moist, ripe flavours lie in this traditional Italian bread salad.

I day-old ciabatta loaf, crusts
  removed and cubed

3 cloves garlic, crushed

2 tblsp red wine vinegar

1/4–1/2 cup extra virgin olive oil

sea salt and freshly ground black pepper

6 Roma tomatoes, diced

I red onion, peeled and diced

2 red peppers, roasted and sliced
  or 1/2 cup sliced pimientos

1/4 cup capers

1/2 cup pitted black olives or Olivelle

1/4–1/2 cup chopped fresh basil

1   Place bread into a bowl, cover with water and leave to soak for 10 minutes until spongy. Squeeze bread with your hands to remove as much water as possible then crumble into coarse, textured crumbs.

2   Place crumbled bread into a large salad bowl. Blend together garlic, vinegar and olive oil to form a dressing. Season with salt and pepper to taste. Pour dressing over bread and toss well.

3   Add diced tomatoes and red onion, peppers or pimientos, capers, olives and basil to the bread and toss well. Serve at room temperature.

SERVES 6

DELI SANDWICH WITH BACON, EGG & SALSA VERDE
This hot bacon and egg theme sandwich is perfect for brunch

1/2 cup salsa verde (see page 92)

4–8 rindless slices of bacon

3 eggs

3 tblsp cold water

salt and pepper

olive oil

4 small finger rolls or ficelle

1 Prepare salsa verde. Grill bacon until crisp; drain on paper towels.
2 Break eggs into a bowl and lightly beat with 3 tblsp cold water; season with salt and pepper. Heat a small frying pan with a little olive oil. Pour in egg mixture and cook into an omelette by drawing in the egg mixture from the sides of the pan until egg is just cooked. Remove to a board and slice into strips.
3 Slice rolls and fill with hot bacon and strips of omelette. Dollop salsa verde over filling.

MAKES 4

BREAD STUFFING OF QUINCE & ORANGE
Delicious stuffing, whether roasted, packed inside a chicken or as a separate vegetarian loaf, makes for a very comforting meal.

4 cups fresh breadcrumbs, loosely
  packed (I like to use wholegrain bread)

3 tblsp olive oil

2 cloves garlic, crushed

I onion, finely chopped

1/4–1/2 cup finely chopped fresh herbs
  (try parsley, sage, thyme, oregano or
  a mixture)

grated zest of I orange

1/4 cup quince paste, roughly chopped

I egg, beaten

salt and freshly ground black pepper

1 Cut crusts off sliced bread and place into the bowl of a food processor. Process to form crumbs.
2 Heat a pan and sweat onion and garlic in olive oil until soft and translucent but not coloured. Mix in bread off the heat. Transfer to a bowl to cool.
3 Once cold, mix in herbs, orange zest and quince paste. Stir in beaten egg to bind stuffing and season with salt and pepper to taste.
4 Pack stuffing into a chicken and roast in the usual manner (see fragrant chicken, page 114) or bake separately in a greased loaf tin at 190°C for 30–40 minutes or until golden brown.

MAKES ENOUGH STUFFING
FOR 1 CHICKEN OR 1 LOAF

DELI SANDWICH WITH BACON, EGG & SALSA VERDE

GRISSINI

Grissini are wonderfully crisp thin bread sticks that are perfect to serve alongside bowls of dips or a mixed antipasto platter.

I tblsp active yeast
1/4 cup warm water
2 cups high grade or Tipo '00' flour
1/2 tsp salt
1/4 tsp chilli powder
2 tblsp olive oil
1/2 cup warm water
I tblsp sea salt flakes
fennel or poppy seeds (optional)

1   Mix yeast into 1/4 cup warm water and leave for 5 minutes to activate and foam.
2   Place flour, salt and chilli powder into a large bowl. Mix in activated yeast mixture, oil and 1/2 cup warm water to form a smooth dough. Knead for 5 minutes then place into a lightly oiled bowl. Cover with plastic wrap and leave in a warm place for about 1 hour or until doubled in bulk.
3   Heat oven to 190°C and lightly oil two baking trays.
4   Knock back dough with your fist and knead lightly. Divide into 20 even-sized pieces. Roll each piece into a long thin strip and place onto prepared trays.
5   Sprinkle with sea salt flakes and fennel or poppy seeds if desired and bake for 10 minutes until crisp and golden brown. Remove to a wire rack to cool.
6   Serve with a favourite dip such as beetroot, herb or sun-dried tomato hummus (see page 65).

MAKES 20

BREAD & GARLIC CUSTARDS

A meltingly soft garlic centre is hidden under the crisp crusts of these individual bread custards.

1/2 cup milk
12 cloves garlic, peeled
2 bay leaves
2 small eggs
2 tblsp olive oil
1/2 cup cream
2 tblsp chopped fresh sage
sea salt
freshly ground black pepper
8 thick slices white bread,
** crusts removed**
softened butter for tins

1   Place milk, garlic cloves and bay leaves into a saucepan and bring to the boil, then simmer for 5 minutes. Remove bay leaves and purée garlic and milk in a blender. Whisk eggs with oil and cream, then whisk in garlic and milk purée and sage. Season with salt and pepper.
2   Cut bread into even-sized cubes and use to fill 6 buttered 180ml capacity ramekins or muffin tins. Pour custard over bread and leave for at least 10 minutes for liquid to soak into bread.
3   Preheat oven to 180°C. Bake bread custards for 15–20 minutes until puffed and golden. Remove and serve hot as an accompaniment to meat or vegetable dishes.

SERVES 6

PANETTONE TOASTED SANDWICHES FILLED WITH RAISIN PURÉE & CHOCOLATE

This is a magnificent, bittersweet, toasted sandwich creation.

1/2 cup raisins

1/2 cup rum, whisky or brandy

1/4 cup tightly packed brown sugar

softened butter

8 slices panettone (or substitute sliced brioche)

200g bittersweet chocolate, grated

icing sugar to dust

1 Heat raisins and rum, whisky or brandy in a bowl in the microwave or bring to the boil in a saucepan. Cover and leave to soften overnight.

2 Next day, place the raisins and liquid with the brown sugar in a saucepan and bring to the boil, stirring until sugar dissolves. Simmer briefly until syrupy, then remove to cool. Purée to a smooth paste in a food processor.

3 Lightly butter slices of panettone. Lay out 4 slices, buttered side down, and spread evenly with raisin purée. Sprinkle evenly with grated chocolate and top with remaining slices of panettone, buttered side up.

4 Heat a large non-stick frying pan and fry sandwiches over a medium heat until golden brown on both sides and chocolate has melted. Serve immediately dusted with icing sugar if desired.

SERVES 4

MARMALADE & CHOCOLATE BREAD PUDDING

Aim to combine the tastes and textures of your favourite marmalade with a quality brand of chocolate such as Valrhona.

10 thin slices bread of choice

50g butter, softened

1/2 cup orange marmalade

250g chopped dark chocolate

1/2 cup sultanas

4 large eggs

pinch salt

1 1/2 cups milk

1/2 cup cream

1/2 cup vanilla sugar (see note page 122)

2 tblsp quality cocoa powder

icing sugar to dust

1 Grease a 1.5 litre-capacity ovenproof baking dish.

2 Make marmalade sandwiches with bread, butter and marmalade and cut into triangular quarters. Place firmly in layers in prepared dish, alternating with chopped chocolate and sultanas.

3 Beat eggs, salt, milk, cream, vanilla sugar and cocoa together. Pour evenly over prepared bread, leave to rest for 1/2 hour for bread to completely absorb liquid.

4 Preheat oven to 160°C. Place pudding dish into a large deep oven tray and fill with hot water to come half way up the sides of the pudding dish. Bake for 45 minutes or until set.

5 Dust with icing sugar to serve.

SERVES 8–10

RUM BABAS

Donna Norton-Lodge, this is especially for you my friend as I know how much you love intoxicating Rum Babas! For those who don't know — these are cake-like breads studded with currants, saturated in rum syrup and named after the fabled Ali Baba.

¼ cup warm milk

3 tsp active dried yeast

I tsp sugar

I ½ cups standard plain flour

I tblsp sugar

¼ tsp salt

50g butter, softened

2 small eggs, lightly beaten

¼ cup currants

Rum syrup:

I cup sugar

I ½ cups water

½ cup dark rum (or more if you please)

1 Place warm milk into a small bowl and sprinkle with yeast and 1 tsp sugar. Leave for about 5–10 minutes for yeast to activate and foam.

2 Sift the flour, 1 tblsp sugar and salt into a bowl and make a well in the centre. Pour activated yeast mixture, softened butter and lightly beaten eggs into the well and mix together to form a wet dough. Don't be concerned if the dough is fairly runny.

3 Beat with a dough hook attachment in a mixer or by hand vigorously until smooth and elastic. Stir in currants.

4 Butter a 24cm ring mould or 6 individual ring moulds. Fill with dough to no more than half full. Cover with plastic wrap and leave in a warm place for about 1 hour or until doubled in size.

5 Bake in a preheated oven at 190°C for 25 minutes or 15 minutes for individual moulds.

6 Meanwhile, to make the rum syrup, bring sugar and water to the boil in a saucepan, stirring until sugar dissolves. Simmer until syrupy. Remove from heat and stir in rum.

7 Turn out Babas onto a plate. Prick all over and saturate with rum syrup.

SERVES 6

RUM BABAS

JAM OF PINK WATERMELON WITH BAGELS

DOUGHNUT ICE-CREAM SANDWICHES

This is a decadent cross between a hot ice-cream sandwich and a cinnamon cream doughnut! Home-made cinnamon ice-cream is extremely easy to make and very special, but you could cheat and buy some ice-cream while at the deli.

6 quality doughnuts, split in half

Cinnamon ice-cream:
4 whole eggs
1/2 cup sugar
2 tblsp ground cinnamon
2 tblsp Amaretto liqueur
2 cups cream, lightly whipped

1   Whisk eggs and sugar together in a cake mixer for at least 10 minutes until very thick and pale and until lifted spoonfuls of mixture fall in ribbons.
2   Fold in cinnamon, liqueur and cream. Pour into a 1 litre plastic container and cover tightly. Freeze overnight. This makes more than you'll need for 6 servings but lasts for up to 3 months in the freezer.
3   Toast or grill doughnut halves on both sides and sandwich together with scoops of cinnamon ice-cream.

SERVES 6

JAM OF PINK WATERMELON WITH BAGELS

Bagels are very fashionable. Try them fresh or toasted, with avocado and pesto, cheese and chutney, perhaps honeycomb, cream cheese or an exotic jam such as this one.

500g Granny Smith apples, peeled, cored and chopped
juice of 3 lemons
2 cups sugar
1/2 cup water
750g pink watermelon flesh, seeds removed, chopped

1   Place apples, lemon juice, sugar and water into a large saucepan or preserving pan and bring to the boil, stirring until sugar dissolves.
2   Simmer for 15–20 minutes then add watermelon. Cook for a further 15–20 minutes or until mixture is thick and jammy.
3   Pour into hot sterilised jars and seal well. Store in the fridge after opening.
4   Spoon liberally onto hot toasted bagels.

MAKES ABOUT 5 CUPS

STICKY SUGAR BUNS

STICKY SUGAR BUNS

This much sought-after recipe comes with a firm warning — sticky sugar buns are downright dangerous! I cannot take any responsibility for what might happen if you choose to make them.

These particular sticky buns are a creation based on an ancient French delicacy, which I have flavoured and adapted. People come from far and wide when the sticky-delicious-caramel scent of these buns is on the wind. However, an obsession with these sticky buns has caused people to lose their integrity, betray friends, behave irrationally, fight over the last one and come close to rioting and rudeness when suffering from withdrawal symptoms. So, please note — sticky sugar buns are an addictive substance. They may ruin your oven, your waistline and probably your cholesterol levels. Make and eat them at your own risk. You have been warned!

STICKY SUGAR BUNS

I tsp sugar
2 tblsp active dry yeast
1⁄2 cup warm water
3 cups high grade or Tipo '00' flour
I tsp salt
1⁄4 cup light, fruity olive oil
I 1⁄4 cups warm milk
extra flour for rolling dough
150g butter, well softened
1 3⁄4 cups caster sugar
flavouring of choice (below)
extra butter to grease tins
icing sugar to dust

Flavouring options:
I tblsp cinnamon and 1⁄2 cup
  raisins, sultanas or currants
1⁄2 cup chopped dried apricots
1⁄2 cup ground almonds
1⁄2 cup desiccated coconut
1⁄2 cup chocolate chips

1. Sprinkle sugar and yeast over 1⁄2 cup warm water and leave to activate for about 5 minutes until foaming.
2. Place flour and salt into a large bowl and make a well in the centre.
3. Pour activated yeast mixture, olive oil and warm milk into the well and bring together with your hand to form a smooth dough. Knead for a few minutes. This dough is best left overnight in a bowl and covered with plastic wrap.
4. Next day, lightly knead dough with a little extra flour. Roll out onto a well-floured surface to form a large rectangle. Cover surface of dough evenly with 3⁄4 of the measured malleable butter in a thick layer. Sprinkle 1 cup of measured sugar evenly over butter and scatter chosen flavouring over sugar.
5. Fold the bottom one-third of dough lengthways up onto the centre one-third and the top one-third of dough lengthways down onto this (like a piece of paper folded in 3.)
6. Dust with more flour and roll out this shape of dough again to form a similar-sized rectangle to step 4. Cover surface with remaining butter and sugar in the same manner. Now, roll this up into a long log.
7. Grease a 12-hole standard muffin pan with butter. Slice pin-wheel roll into 12 even portions and place into tins with spiral facing upwards.
8. Place muffin pan into a larger baking pan to catch any sugary drips and bake for 30 minutes in an oven heated to 200°C. Remove from pans quickly or sticky toffee will set. Best served warm dusted with lots of icing sugar.

MAKES 12

I have developed several delicious flavourings for these sticky sugar bun creations. Many people will happily eat any of them but some people have a firm favourite (mine is apricot). There are other possibilities but I have found that these additions work best with the texture of the buns.

BAGEL – Jewish speciality bread roll with a hole in the centre. The unique texture of bagels is due to the process whereby they are boiled before being baked.

BAGUETTE – classic French loaf, long and thin with a thick and beautifully crisp crust.

BRIOCHE – sweet cake-like yeasted bread enriched with eggs and butter. May be baked in the form of a loaf or individual fluted shapes.

BRUSCHETTA – slices of bread that are chargrilled then drizzled with olive oil and rubbed with garlic and eaten as is or used as a base for toppings.

CIABATTA – flat, slipper-shaped Italian loaf of bread with an airy texture inside and a pale, crisp crust sometimes dusted with flour.

CROSTINI – small pieces of dry toasted bread, sometimes lightly oiled before baking and used as a base for toppings.

FICELLE – small and very thin stick of French bread.

FLAT BREAD – many different cultures have their own version of this simple yet varied form of bread, for example, pita from the Middle East or tortillas from Mexico. See also focaccia and pide.

FOCACCIA – yeasted flat bread with a dimpled surface drizzled with olive oil and sprinkled with sea salt and sometimes herbs.

GRISSINI – Italian crisp bread sticks.

PAIN AU LEVAIN – bread leavened with natural airborne yeasts.

PANETTONE – rich cake-like celebration bread of Italy containing dried fruits, citrus peel and spices. Panettone are baked in special paper cases and can be found in attractive boxes in delicatessens around Christmas time.

PIDE – Turkish flat bread that may have yoghurt as an ingredient and is sometimes scattered with sesame seeds.

PITA – Middle Eastern round or oval flat bread that puffs to form a hollow pocket inside the bread. Pita pockets can be filled or sliced and toasted to serve with dips.

SODA BREAD – soft loaf of bread raised with bicarbonate of soda instead of yeast.

SOURDOUGH – bread raised using wild yeasts and involving a long fermentation resulting in a characteristic sour flavour.

TIPO '00' FLOUR – Italian finely ground flour that has a more fragrant flavour; can be used any time fine flour is required.

WHOLEMEAL/WHOLE WHEAT BREAD – brown bread with a more fibrous texture than white bread due to the flour which still contains parts of the whole wheat berry, including some wheatgerm and bran.

02:THE DAIRY

  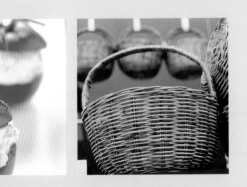

There are just so many superb dairy products available today. Delicatessens and supermarket fridges are brimming with more recent dairy discoveries including mascarpone, quark, bocconcini, haloumi, and ewes' and goats' cheeses. The recipes in this chapter exploit the versatility and unique characteristics of some of these dairy products in cooking.

The best advice I can give as to which cheeses you might prefer to cook with is to make a visit to a speciality cheese shop or investigate the cheese room in a delicatessen. Here you can smell and taste the cheeses, and this will help you learn how they differ and which flavours and textures you like. You will probably find that with time and varied taste experiences you will develop a liking for more and more unusual cheeses.

DOUBLE-BAKED CHEESE SOUFFLÉS

Soufflés, while popular with many people, are often avoided because of their reputed difficulty. This double-baked method alleviates all concerns because there is no chance of deflation or last-minute cooking hassles.

I cup milk

2 bay leaves

75g butter

1/4 cup flour

sea salt

pinch cayenne pepper

2 eggs, separated

125g Gruyère cheese, grated

I cup cream

1/2 cup freshly grated
   Parmigiano-Reggiano

1 Place milk and bay leaves into a saucepan and heat until just about to boil. Remove from heat and set aside to infuse and cool, then strain.

2 Heat oven to 180°C. Grease 6 3/4-cup capacity ramekins and place these onto an oven tray.

3 Melt butter in a saucepan and stir in flour off the heat to form a smooth paste. Return to heat and cook for 1–2 minutes, stirring constantly. Remove from heat and stir in milk until smooth. Bring to the boil, stirring until mixture thickens. Season with salt and pinch of cayenne pepper. Transfer to a bowl, stir in egg yolks and Gruyère cheese.

4 In a clean bowl, whisk egg whites until soft peaks form. Gently fold egg whites into cheese mixture.

5 Spoon into ramekins and bake for 20 minutes until puffed. Remove to cool until ready to serve. Soufflés can be made ahead and refrigerated for 2–3 days.

6 Turn soufflés out into 6 individual, small, shallow ovenproof dishes. Pour some cream over each and sprinkle with Parmesan. Bake in a preheated oven for 20 minutes or until golden brown.

SERVES 6

MASCARPONE, LEEK & FETA TARTS

The unpretentious leek is elevated to great heights via this creamy pie filling which is an adaptation of a recipe from my friend and talented cook, Jennifer LeComte.

400g savoury short-crust pastry

1 Roll out pastry to 3mm thick and line 8 individual 10cm tart tins. Prick bases and chill well.

2 Line pastry cases with non-stick baking paper and fill with baking beans to bake blind. Place tart tins onto a baking tray and cook for 15 minutes in an oven heated to 200°C. Remove paper and beans.

Filling:
3 leeks, trimmed
3 tblsp olive oil
1½ cups mascarpone (or substitute sour cream)
3 eggs, lightly beaten
1 tblsp chopped thyme
½ cup pitted Kalamata or other black olives
salt and freshly ground black pepper

1 Finely slice leeks, wash and drain well. In a saucepan sweat leeks in olive oil until softened but not browned. Remove to a bowl to cool.

2 Stir in mascarpone, eggs, thyme, olives and salt and pepper to taste. Spoon into prepared pastry shells.

3 Bake at 180°C for 20–25 minutes or until filling is golden and just set.

SERVES 8

MASCARPONE & PARSNIP PURÉE

This versatile purée can be served hot as a vegetable dish or cold as a sumptuous dip.

2 large (about 500g) parsnips, peeled
4 cloves garlic
¾ cup mascarpone (or substitute sour cream)
pinch freshly grated nutmeg
salt and freshly ground black pepper

1 Roughly chop parsnips into even-sized pieces. Cook in boiling salted water with whole garlic cloves for 20 minutes or until tender. Drain well and cool a little.

2 Purée parsnips and garlic in a food processor, then add mascarpone and blend until smooth. Season with nutmeg, and salt and pepper to taste.

3 Serve chilled as a dip or spread, or reheat to serve as a hot vegetable accompaniment.

MAKES 2 CUPS

YOGHURT CHEESE

This strained yoghurt is also known by the Middle Eastern name of labneh. The rolled balls can be dipped in herbs, seeds or spices and nibbled as a snack. They're also excellent tossed in a salad or served as a creamy, cooling accompaniment to spicy dishes.

large square of fine muslin or cheesecloth

4 cups natural yoghurt

I tsp fine sea salt

optional flavourings of choice (see method)

1   Sterilise a piece of muslin or cheesecloth by boiling in a saucepan of water for 5 minutes. Cool and squeeze out excess moisture.

2   Spread out muslin in a large bowl and pour yoghurt into the centre. Add salt. Leave plain or stir in flavourings of choice such as chopped garlic, herbs, saffron threads, sesame seeds to taste.

3   Bring the four corners of muslin together and tie them around a wooden spoon. Suspend the spoon over the bowl and allow the yoghurt to drain in the fridge for 2–3 days.

4   After 2 days the yoghurt cheese is thick and spreadable. After 3 days the cheese is firm and can be rolled into balls, which will keep for about 10 days in the fridge, marinated in olive oil.

MAKES ABOUT 2 CUPS

BAKED SAVOURY RICOTTA

Plain baked ricotta is nice and can be accompanied by a flavoursome salsa or chutney. Alternatively, infuse with saffron, chilli, lemon and basil for a version that is fragrant in itself.

500g ricotta

2 eggs, lightly beaten

1/4 tsp saffron threads

I red chilli, seeds removed and finely chopped

finely grated rind of I lemon

3 tblsp chopped fresh basil

3 cloves garlic, crushed

salt to taste

1   Preheat oven to 180°C. Oil an 18cm spring-form cake tin and line the base with non-stick baking paper.

2   Mix ricotta with remaining ingredients and pour into prepared tin.

3   Bake for 40 minutes or until golden brown and set. Remove to cool in the tin.

4   Remove set baked ricotta from tin and cut into wedges to serve.

SERVES 4

GOATS' CHEESE STUFFED VINE TOMATOES

I'm not usually one to sit around stuffing miniature vegetables — life is too short! But for some reason these tomatoes with their perfect shape and ripeness and their perfect calyx beg to be left to show off their pretty form. Plus they are totally delicious!

12 small vine-ripened tomatoes

100g soft goats' cheese

finely grated rind and juice of 1 lemon

2 tblsp snipped fresh chives

salt and freshly ground black pepper

1   Cut tops off tomatoes and scoop out the seeds to form cups.
2   Mash goats' cheese with the remaining ingredients and pipe or spoon into hollowed-out tomatoes and replace tops.
3   Serve cherry tomatoes as finger food and small tomatoes as an entrée.
4   Small tomatoes can also be baked in a hot oven for 10 minutes drizzled with a little olive oil. Serve hot with crusty bread.

MAKES 12

SMOKED HAVARTI, SAGE & POTATO PIE

Havarti is a cheese that has a luxurious creamy texture and rich flavour. The smoked form is even more full-flavoured, but any smoked cheese would make an acceptable substitute.

400g savoury short crust pastry

1.2kg waxy potatoes, peeled and cooked

200g smoked creamy havarti cheese

2 tblsp finely chopped fresh sage

salt and freshly ground black pepper

3 eggs

¾ cup milk

¼ cup cream

1 beaten egg for glaze

1   Roll out two-thirds of the pastry to 3mm thick and use to line a greased 22cm spring-form cake tin. Cut potatoes and cheese into ½cm slices and arrange in layers alternating with a sprinkling of chopped sage and salt and pepper to season. Firmly press down filling.
2   Beat eggs with milk and cream and pour over filling. Roll out remaining pastry and use to cover pie. Press pastry edges together to seal, trim excess and decorate as desired. Make small cuts in pastry top to release steam.
3   Glaze with beaten egg and bake for 1 hour in an oven heated to 190°C. Cover with foil if necessary to prevent pastry becoming too brown.

SERVES 8

GOATS' CHEESE STUFFED VINE TOMATOES

GORGONZOLA LIMA BEANS

I find this dish very pleasing. Soft lima beans, in a way, take the place of pasta and cling blissfully to the Gorgonzola sauce.

1 1/2 cups dried lima beans, soaked
   overnight in plenty of cold water
1/2 cup cream
200g Gorgonzola cheese
salt and freshly ground black pepper
1/4 cup fresh sage leaves

1 Drain soaking water from beans, place beans into a saucepan and cover with fresh cold water. Bring to the boil, then cover and simmer for 1 hour or until beans are tender. Drain well.
2 Place cream and Gorgonzola into a saucepan and heat until cheese melts. Cook for a few minutes until thickened to form a creamy sauce. Stir in hot beans and season with salt and pepper to taste.
3 Chop fresh sage and add or, if you like, fry whole sage leaves in a little olive oil until crisp. Drain on paper towels and sprinkle over Gorgonzola lima beans.

SERVES 4 AS AN ENTRÉE

HALOUMI & PEPPER SALAD

Haloumi is typically sliced then grilled or fried, but I find small cubes are a particularly appealing and tactile way to present this unusual cheese.

2 red peppers, seeds removed, sliced
2 yellow peppers, seeds removed, sliced
olive oil for frying
200g haloumi cheese, cut into
   5mm cubes
2 cups washed baby spinach leaves
1/4 cup salted capers, rinsed
   and drained
2 cloves garlic, chopped
1 tblsp chopped fresh rosemary
finely grated zest and juice of 1 lemon
3 tblsp extra virgin olive oil
salt and freshly ground black pepper

1 Toss peppers in olive oil and stir-fry in a hot frypan for about 5 minutes or until charred and slightly caramelised. Place into a large bowl.
2 Add a little more olive oil to the pan and fry haloumi cubes for a few minutes, tossing until browned all over. Drain on paper towels then add to bowl with peppers and toss in spinach.
3 Blend together capers, garlic, rosemary, lemon juice, zest and olive oil and season with salt and pepper to taste. Pour dressing over salad ingredients and toss well. Serve immediately.

SERVES 4

PARMESAN PARSLEY DUST

This vivid green sprinkle can be used as both a flavoursome topping and an attractive garnish to many foods. Try it scattered over pasta dishes, salads and soups or dust casually over trays of finger food to decorate.

1/2 cup tightly packed parsley
leaves, dried with paper towels
1/2 cup freshly grated
Parmigiano-Reggiano

1 Place parsley into the bowl of a food processor and pulse to chop.
2 Add Parmesan and process until green crumbs form.
3 Sprinkle dust over food as desired for colour and flavour or to decorate.

MAKES 3/4 CUP

BLUE CHEESE, CHICKEN & BROCCOLI GRATIN

A long time ago now, my very dear friend, Jane Arbuthnott, who is a brilliant cook, kindly shared this special recipe with me. It is a striking combination, which I continue to enjoy cooking and eating today.

olive oil
500g chicken breasts, cut into
thick slices
3 tblsp olive oil
2 tblsp flour
1 1/2 cups chicken stock
1 tblsp chopped fresh oregano
or marjoram
1 cup sour cream
75g blue cheese, crumbled
salt and freshly ground black pepper
1 head broccoli, cut into florets and
blanched, or 1 bunch broccolini,
blanched
50g butter
1/2 cup fresh breadcrumbs

1 Heat a frying pan with a little oil and lightly brown chicken on both sides but do not overcook. Remove to one side.
2 Add 3 tblsp olive oil to pan and stir in flour to form a smooth paste. Cook over gentle heat, stirring, for a few minutes. Blend in stock off the heat. Return to the heat, stirring constantly until sauce thickens.
3 Add oregano, sour cream and blue cheese to melt. Season with salt and pepper to taste. Mix in broccoli and prepared chicken and pour into an ovenproof dish.
4 Bake in an oven preheated to 180°C for 30 minutes.
5 Meanwhile, heat butter in a small frying pan, mix in breadcrumbs and cook over a medium heat until crumbs are golden brown and crisp. Sprinkle crumbs on top of cooked chicken dish to complete.
6 Parmesan parsley dust (see above) also makes a nice addition to this crumb topping.

SERVES 4

BLUE CHEESE, CHICKEN & BROCCOLI GRATIN WITH PARMESAN PARSLEY DUST

MARINATED BOCCONCINI

MARINATED BOCCONCINI

Alternative cheeses that also work well in this marinade are feta, chèvre and strained yoghurt cheese.

2 cloves garlic

1/2 cup parsley leaves, tightly packed

1/4 cup basil leaves, tightly packed

3/4 cup extra virgin olive oil

1/2 tsp cracked black pepper

I tsp fennel seeds, toasted

pared rind of I lemon

300g bocconcini (baby mozzarella balls), drained from whey

1 Purée garlic and herbs with oil, add pepper, fennel seeds and lemon rind. Place bocconcini in a jar and pour over marinade. Refrigerate overnight so that flavours infuse.

2 Bring to room temperature before serving with bread, in a salad or as part of an antipasto.

MAKES 2 CUPS

SWEET RICOTTA CAKE

Any soft curd cheese such as ricotta, quark, fromage frais or a mixture of these can be used interchangeably in this delightfully subtle, light-textured cheesecake.

150g butter

I 1/2 cups sugar

4 eggs, separated

600g ricotta

I tsp vanilla extract

finely grated zest and juice of 2 lemons

3/4 cup semolina

1/2 cup ground almonds, plus extra for dusting

1/2 cup dried currants

1 Preheat oven to 160ºC. Grease a 20cm spring-form cake tin and dust with extra ground almonds.

2 Cream butter and sugar until pale. Beat in egg yolks, ricotta, vanilla, lemon zest and juice. Fold in semolina, ground almonds and currants and mix well.

3 Whisk egg whites to soft peaks and gently fold into cake mixture.

4 Pour into prepared cake tin. Bake for 20 minutes or until a skewer inserted comes out clean.

SERVES 10

BOCCONCINI – small balls of mozzarella cheese stored in whey so that they remain moist and fresh.

CHÈVRE – goats' milk cheese that has a distinctive earthy and slightly sharp flavour.

FETA – fresh cheese that is pressed, sliced and preserved stored in brine. Traditionally feta was made with ewes' or goats' milk but is now regularly and successfully made with cows' milk.

FROMAGE FRAIS – fresh cultured milk cheese with a slight citrus tang.

GRANA PADANO – hard grainy cheese also commonly known as Parmesan and used in the same way.

PARMESAN – see also Parmigiano-Reggiano and Grana Padano. Parmesan is best bought fresh and eaten as part of a cheese board, grated or shaved over food.

GORGONZOLA – from Lombardy, Italy, this rich cheese has a sharp flavour from its blue-green marbling of mould.

HALOUMI – originally a sheep's milk cheese from Cyprus, now often made with cows' milk. This stretched curd cheese is stored in light brine and typically served fried or grilled. Haloumi has a firm, chewy texture.

MASCARPONE – technically not a curd cheese but a cultured cream made in much the same way as yoghurt. Mascarpone has a voluptuous thick creamy texture and can be used in sweet and savoury recipes.

LABNEH – Middle Eastern name for strained yoghurt that thickens to form a type of fresh cheese. May be seen written as labna or labne.

MOZZARELLA – stretched fresh curd cheese that melts to an elastic consistency. Mozzarella has a subtle flavour so is often used to add texture to dishes.

PARMIGIANO-REGGIANO – commonly known as Parmesan, a grainy textured, almost fruity/salty flavoured hard cheese from the Emilia Romagna region of Italy.

PECORINO – a family of sheep's milk cheeses with a distinct piquant flavour.

RICOTTA – a cheese produced from whey. Ricotta is drained in baskets to produce a mass of fine, moist grains.

SOFT-WHITE CHEESES – creamy smooth cheeses with a mould rind, such as Brie and Camembert.

QUARK – a low-fat, fresh curd cheese with a lemon-fresh acidic tartness.

THE PANTRY SHELVES OF DELICATESSENS ARE CRAMMED WITH JARS OF WONDERFUL FLAVOURS AND CONDIMENTS, FOR EXAMPLE PESTOS, CHUTNEYS AND PICKLES; PRESERVED ITEMS SUCH AS SUN-DRIED TOMATOES AND OTHER PRESERVED VEGETABLES LIKE ARTICHOKE HEARTS AND PIMIENTOS. THEN THERE ARE EVEN MORE EXCEPTIONAL PRODUCTS SUCH AS TRUFFLES, ANCHOVIES AND DRIED PORCINI TO INVESTIGATE AND ENJOY. TRANSPORT THESE PRODUCTS FROM THE SHELVES OF THE DELI TO THE SHELVES OF YOUR OWN PANTRY — THEY ARE USEFUL AND VERSATILE INGREDIENTS TO HAVE ON HAND. HERE ARE SOME RECIPES TO WIDEN YOUR REPERTOIRE AND TO HELP EXTEND OR USE UP THOSE JARS OF GOODIES THAT YOU MAY NOT HAVE PREVIOUSLY KNOWN QUITE WHAT TO DO WITH.

ANCHOVY, ALMOND-CRUSTED LAMB RACKS WITH MASCARPONE & PARSNIP PURÉE

ANCHOÏADE

Anchoïade is basically a paste of pounded fleshy anchovies and is served as a spread or used to flavour other preparations such as mayonnaise, vinaigrettes or marinades.

150g quality anchovy fillets

2 cloves garlic, peeled

3–4 tblsp extra virgin olive oil

1 tblsp wine or sherry vinegar
  or lemon juice

freshly ground black pepper

1 Pound together anchovies and garlic in a mortar and pestle or purée in a food processor until a paste is formed.

2 Blend in oil and vinegar or lemon juice to amalgamate, and season with pepper to taste.

MAKES 1/2 CUP

ANCHOVY, ALMOND-CRUSTED LAMB RACKS

This crunchy crust spiked with the tang of anchovies creates a beautiful contrast to the sweetness of lamb.

3 tblsp anchoïade

1/4 cup finely chopped parsley

1 cup ground almonds

2 egg whites, lightly beaten

4 baby lamb racks, French trimmed

salt and freshly ground black pepper

1 Heat oven to 190°C. Mix anchoïade with parsley, ground almonds and egg whites and press evenly onto outside of lamb racks. Place lamb racks in an oven pan and season with salt and pepper to taste.

2 Roast in preheated oven for 20 minutes for medium rare. Remove to rest for 10 minutes before serving.

3 Serve 1 lamb rack per person.

SERVES 4

CRUMBED ARTICHOKES WITH MOSTARDA DI FRUTTA SALSA

CRUMBED ARTICHOKES

These days there are not many foods that I would deep fry, but crumbed artichokes are a special treat and make a particularly good finger food item.

2 cups quality artichoke hearts

I egg

pinch salt

I cup dry breadcrumbs

salt and freshly ground black pepper

olive oil for frying

1 Drain artichokes and dry on paper towels.
2 Lightly beat egg in a bowl with a little salt. Season breadcrumbs with salt and pepper and place on a tray.
3 Dip artichoke hearts first in egg and then in crumbs. Press crumbs on well to coat.
4 Place 5cm depth of olive oil in a heavy-based pan and heat for frying. Test heat by dropping a cube of bread into oil – it should bubble and turn golden brown. Fry crumbed artichokes in batches for 2–3 minutes or until golden brown and crisp. Drain on paper towels.
5 Serve hot or cold.

SERVES 4–6 AS A SNACK OR FINGER FOOD

LAMB SHANKS WITH SUN-DRIED TOMATOES & MUSHROOMS

Long, slow, moist cooking is the key to perfect lamb shanks. In this recipe, sun-dried tomatoes melt into the sauce and impart their concentrated flavour.

8 small lamb shanks, trimmed

2 red onions, finely diced

6 slices rindless bacon, chopped

3 cloves garlic, chopped

I tblsp sweet smoked Spanish paprika

4 bay leaves

I tblsp chopped fresh marjoram or oregano

I cup red wine

2 1/2 cups beef stock

I cup sun-dried tomatoes, drained from oil

200g button mushrooms, halved

salt and freshly ground black pepper

1 Preheat oven to 170ºC. Season lamb shanks and place into a roasting pan to fit snugly and cover with remaining ingredients, except sun-dried tomatoes and mushrooms.
2 Cover pan, place into oven and bake for 2 hours, turning once, until lamb is tender.
3 Add sun-dried tomatoes and mushrooms, stirring to combine. Return to the oven uncovered and bake for a further 40 minutes. Check and adjust seasoning if necessary before serving.

SERVES 4–6

FREE-FORM SAVOURY TART

SUN-DRIED TOMATO SCRAMBLED EGGS

Good scrambled eggs are a great way to start the day, especially on the weekend.

4 eggs
¼ cup cream (or milk, but
  cream is best)
salt and freshly ground black pepper
½ cup sun-dried tomatoes,
  drained and sliced
25g butter
4 tblsp prepared basil pesto

1 Beat eggs together with cream or milk, adding salt and a generous grinding of pepper to season. Stir in sun-dried tomato slices.
2 Melt butter in a large saucepan and pour in egg mixture to cook over a medium heat. As the egg sets around the edges draw the set egg into the centre with a wooden spoon. Repeat folding until mixture is mostly set but still moist.
3 Spoon onto freshly toasted bread or bagels and top with a good dollop of pesto.

SERVES 2–4 DEPENDING ON HOW HUNGRY YOU ARE

FREE-FORM SAVOURY TART

This savoury tart is truly scrumptious and incorporates a medley of pantry products, which can be varied according to whatever you have on hand.

Pastry:
2 cups flour
1 tsp Spanish smoked bittersweet
  paprika
½ tsp salt
150g butter, cut into cubes
3 tblsp ice-cold water

Filling:
¼ cup basil pesto
200g canned tuna, roughly drained
  and flaked
½ cup chopped sun-dried tomatoes
½ cup torn fresh basil leaves
6 fresh tomatoes, sliced
½ cup pitted black olives
½ cup artichoke hearts, sliced
sea salt and freshly ground black pepper

1 Heat oven to 200°C. To make pastry, place flour, paprika and salt into a bowl. Rub butter into dry ingredients until a fine crumb texture forms.
2 Add just enough ice-cold water to form a firm dough when brought together.
3 Roll out pastry to form a large circle 3mm thick and transfer to a lightly oiled baking tray.
4 Layer filling ingredients onto pastry leaving a 3cm rim. Fold rim over outer circumference of filling to form a secure edge. Brush pastry edges with egg wash (1 egg yolk mixed with a little salt and milk).
5 Bake in preheated oven for 25–30 minutes or until pastry is golden brown.

SERVES 10

PORCINI GRAVY WITH VENISON

A powder of porcini mushrooms is also available from some delicatessens; this can be used to flavour sauces, stews or soups. Meats can be rolled in porcini powder before roasting, or dusted with the powder before searing in a hot pan.

15g dried porcini mushrooms

700g venison loin, trimmed

olive oil

1 cup well-reduced beef or
  venison stock

1/4 cup sherry

salt and freshly ground black pepper

1 Just cover dried porcini with warm water and leave to soak for 30 minutes. Slice venison into 8–12 medallions.

2 Heat a pan and sear venison medallions briefly in a little oil to brown on both sides. Do not overcook or venison will be dry. Remove to rest and keep warm while preparing the gravy.

3 Place beef or venison stock and sherry into a saucepan, bring to the boil, then simmer to reduce and thicken. Add porcini and the soaking liquid and simmer to reduce to a sauce consistency. Adjust seasoning with salt and pepper to taste. Serve over venison.

SERVES 4

WILD FOREST MUSHROOM CHICKEN

This recipe involves a simple method that produces a dish full of sensational, rich earthy flavours.

40g dried wild forest mushrooms

1 cup warm water

6 large chicken legs

4 cloves garlic, peeled and chopped

3 thick slices bacon, roughly chopped

1 tblsp olive oil

1/2 cup pinot noir

1 cup reduced beef stock

1 cup tomato purée

1 heaped tblsp brown sugar

1/4 cup quality balsamic vinegar

1 tblsp arrowroot or cornflour,
  dissolved in a little cold water

salt and freshly ground black pepper

1–2 tblsp extra balsamic vinegar

2 tblsp truffle-infused olive oil (optional)

1 Soak dried mushrooms in warm water for 20 minutes then drain well, strain and reserve liquid. Joint and skin the chicken legs.

2 Heat a heavy-based ovenproof saucepan or casserole. Cook garlic and bacon in oil over a medium heat to lightly brown.

3 Add wine to deglaze the pan and simmer for 5 minutes. Add mushroom water, stock, tomato purée, brown sugar and balsamic vinegar, bring to the boil then simmer for 5 minutes. Pour in dissolved arrowroot or cornflour and stir until mixture thickens.

4 Add the mushrooms and chicken, turning to coat in the sauce. Cook uncovered for 40 minutes in an oven preheated to 170°C, stirring once during cooking. Season with salt and pepper to taste.

5 Finish by stirring in extra balsamic vinegar and truffle oil.

SERVES 6

PORCINI GRAVY WITH VENISON ON PIMIENTO MASH

GHERKIN, ARTICHOKE & ROAST CARROT SALAD

This salad is a pleasant blend of pantry ingredients and common garden vegetables.

4 red onions, peeled

I bunch baby carrots, trimmed, or
  4 large carrots, thickly sliced

olive oil

3 cloves garlic, crushed

salt and freshly ground black pepper

I cup gherkins, cut into thick slices

I cup artichoke hearts, drained from oil

1/2 cup sliced pimientos or roasted
  red peppers

3 tblsp quality balsamic vinegar

1/4 cup extra virgin olive oil

1 Cut onions into wedges and place in a roasting pan with carrots. Drizzle with olive oil and toss with garlic to coat; season with salt and pepper.

2 Roast at 190°C for 20–30 minutes, turning occasionally until caramelised. Remove to a large bowl to cool.

3 Once cold, add gherkins, artichoke hearts and pimientos to the bowl. Drizzle with balsamic vinegar and olive oil and toss well to combine.

SERVES 4–6

MOSTARDA DI FRUTTA SALSA

Mustard fruits are appetising in themselves, but if you're looking for interesting, alternative ways to serve them then the addition of gherkins, lemon and basil elevates them to another level of freshness and flavour.

1/2 cup Mostarda di Frutta
  (Italian mustard fruits)

3 tblsp chopped fresh basil

3 gherkins, finely diced

3 cloves garlic, peeled and chopped

finely grated zest of I lemon

I tblsp lemon juice

salt to taste

1 Drain the liquid from the mustard fruits and reserve. Finely dice mustard fruits and mix with remaining ingredients.

2 Mix some of the reserved liquid back in to moisten salsa.

3 Serve, for example, on top of seared steak, with sliced ham, or to garnish deli-bought toppings such as foie gras on crostini.

MAKES 3/4 CUP

PIMIENTOS STUFFED WITH ANCHOVIES, RICOTTA & PESTO

Piquillo pimientos are a type of small, spicy, sweet pepper that are preserved and found in jars on the deli shelf. Whole, they are the perfect shape to stuff and bake and look a little bit like pretty red hats for pixies!

I cup ricotta

2 cloves garlic, crushed

I tblsp lemon-infused olive oil

finely grated zest of I lemon

6–10 anchovies, roughly chopped

1/4 cup basil pesto

salt and freshly ground black pepper

12 whole Piquillo pimientos, drained

1 Heat oven to 180°C. Mix ricotta with remaining ingredients except pimientos and season with salt and pepper to taste.

2 Pack mixture carefully but firmly into pimientos and place into a baking dish. Bake in a preheated oven for 15 minutes.

MAKES 12

PIMIENTO MASH

A bright modern twist to mash!

Ikg floury potatoes, peeled

1/2 cup pimientos or roasted red peppers

3 tblsp olive oil

milk or cream, heated

salt and freshly ground black pepper

1 Cut potatoes into large, even-sized chunks. Cook in boiling, salted water until tender. Drain potatoes and return to the heat, shaking to dry.

2 Meanwhile, purée pimientos or peppers in a food processor.

3 Mash and sieve or mouli potatoes to remove lumps. Add olive oil, pimiento purée and enough milk or cream to achieve preferred consistency. Season with salt and pepper to taste.

SERVES 6

ANCHOVIES – small, saltwater fish with dark flesh and a distinctive strong flavour, usually sold filleted. The best quality are salt-cured or in olive oil such as Ortiz brand.

ARTICHOKE HEARTS – the fleshy central 'hearts' of immature heads of globe artichokes. The best quality are sold preserved in olive oil.

DRIED FOREST MUSHROOMS – a mixture of European wild forest mushrooms sold dried. They need to be soaked in water to soften for use in cooking. See also porcini (ceps) and mousserons.

GHERKINS – a type of small cucumber that is pickled in a sweet/sour vinegar solution – sometimes known as 'dill pickles'.

MOSTARDA DI FRUTTA – an Italian condiment of various whole candied fruits preserved in a mustard-flavoured sugar syrup; also known as mustard fruits.

MOUSSERONS – one type of dried French wild meadow mushroom that looks like tiny fairy umbrellas.

PESTO – a paste made traditionally from basil, garlic, pinenuts, Parmesan cheese and olive oil ground together and sold bottled in jars. Sometimes other forms of pesto are available such as rocket pesto or sun-dried tomato pesto (paste).

PIMIENTOS – Spanish sweet/spicy peppers preserved in their natural juices or sometimes pickled in a vinegar solution.

PIQUELLO PIMIENTOS – a special variety of pimiento grown in the Navarra region of Spain and recognised as a DOC product. DOC roughly translates to mean 'denomination of control' and is a guarantee of quality and origin of a product.

PORCINI – a type of mushroom (known as 'ceps' in France). Packets of sliced and dried porcini can be purchased from delicatessens. These are strongly flavoured and are soaked in water to re-hydrate; the soaking liquid can also be used in cooking. May also be available in powdered form.

TRUFFLES – a type of fungus, which grows underground in symbiosis with certain trees. This highly prized foodstuff has a powerful earthy aroma and flavour and can be eaten raw or cooked.

THE REFRIGERATED CABINETS IN DELIS HOLD AN ALMOST CONFUSING ARRAY OF MEAT PREPARATIONS, SMOKED POULTRY AND SEAFOODS. YOUR MIND MAY BOGGLE IN WONDERMENT AT THE DIFFERENCE BETWEEN AIR-DRIED THIS AND SALT-CURED THAT. HEREIN LIES ONE OF THE GREATEST ADVANTAGES OF SHOPPING IN SPECIALITY FOOD STORES — THE ASSISTANTS ARE VERY KNOWLEDGEABLE AND UNDERSTAND THEIR PRODUCTS. THEY CAN HELP YOU CHOOSE WHAT PRODUCT IS BEST FOR THE DISH YOU ARE PREPARING. THEY ARE GENERALLY HAPPY TO GIVE OUT SOUND COOKING ADVICE, LITTLE TASTE TESTS AND SOMETIMES EVEN FAVOURITE RECIPES.

SALAMI & CRUNCHY VEGETABLE SALAD

Ask to try before you buy so that you can discover which salami you prefer. A chunky cut shows off the wonderful coarse meaty texture of salami.

I bunch fresh asparagus or beans,
  trimmed and blanched
I green pepper, core and seeds
  removed, diced
I small red onion, peeled and sliced
4 spring onions, trimmed and sliced
1/2 cup stuffed green olives
250g piece of salami, cut into
  large cubes
3 hard-boiled eggs, peeled and chopped
1/4 cup capers, drained
3 tblsp chopped fresh mint leaves
salt and freshly ground black pepper

1   Slice beans or asparagus and toss with remaining salad ingredients. Season with salt and pepper to taste.

Dressing:
1/4 cup extra virgin olive oil
I clove garlic, crushed
I tsp ground coriander seeds
I tsp each whole cumin seeds
  and mustard seeds
I tsp sugar
juice of 2 lemons

1   Heat dressing oil in a pan, add garlic and seeds and cook over a gentle heat, stirring until fragrant. Add sugar and lemon juice and pour dressing over salad. Toss well to combine.

SERVES 4 AS A MAIN

EXOTIC SAUSAGE TAGINE

Try chicken sausages in this exotic stew, or Italian sausages, which contain fennel seeds, or a mix of different-flavoured sausages.

500g quality exotic-flavoured sausages
2 tblsp olive oil
2 onions, peeled and sliced
2 tsp cinnamon
I tblsp grated fresh ginger
3 cloves garlic, peeled and sliced
1/2 cup sherry
200g fresh dates, stones removed
3 cups beef stock
salt and freshly ground black pepper
1/4 cup chopped fresh coriander

1. Heat a large pan and brown sausages in a little oil. Remove to one side.
2. Turn down the heat and gently cook onions in oil for 10 minutes until softened but not coloured. Add cinnamon, ginger and garlic and cook for 1 minute. Add sherry and bring to the boil.
3. Return sausages to the pan and add dates and stock. Bring to the boil then cover and simmer gently for 40 minutes. Skim off any excess fat and season with salt and pepper to taste.
4. Sprinkle with coriander and serve with hot plain buttered couscous or rice if preferred. Serve deli-bought harissa paste on the side if desired.

SERVES 4

CHORIZO & BEEF WITH PRUNES

Chorizo is a fantastic flavour enhancer, lending its spicy taste to this dish, while prunes add a smooth touch of sticky sweetness.

3 tblsp olive oil
750g thick beef sirloin, topside or
  rump steaks, cut into large cubes
4 cloves garlic, chopped
4 chorizo sausages, sliced
3 tblsp flour
I cup red wine
2 cups beef stock
I cup pitted prunes
3 large tomatoes, skinned and
  chopped
1/4 cup capers, drained
2 tblsp chopped fresh oregano
2 bay leaves
salt and freshly ground black pepper

1. Heat a large ovenproof casserole, add oil and brown cubed beef on all sides; remove to one side. Add garlic and chorizo sausage and cook for 2 minutes. Remove from the heat and stir in flour to form a smooth paste.
2. Add wine, stirring to incorporate. Blend in stock and return to the heat. Add prunes, tomatoes, capers, oregano, bay leaf and beef. Bring to the boil, then cover and bake for 45 minutes in an oven preheated to 180°C.
3. Remove covering, skim off any excess fat and season with salt and pepper to taste. Return to oven and cook uncovered for a further 20 minutes.

SERVES 6

SMOKED MUSSEL FRITTERS

Fritters are always popular and these ones are texturally appetising and tasty. Try them with home-made lemon mayonnaise for a special treat.

300g smoked mussels, very
  finely chopped
I egg, lightly beaten
1/3 cup flour
3/4 cup fresh breadcrumbs
I bunch spring onions, very
  finely chopped
1/4 cup finely chopped parsley
salt and freshly ground black pepper
oil for frying
lemon wedges to serve

1 Combine all ingredients in a bowl and mix well. Season with salt and pepper to taste.
2 Heat a heavy-based frying pan, add a little oil and fry tablespoonful lots into fritters, cooking for 1–2 minutes on each side. Drain on paper towels.
3 Serve with lemon wedges on the side.

MAKES 20

SMOKED SALMON & ASPARAGUS SALAD

This salad is simplicity itself to put together; the combined tastes and textures have sensational mouth-appeal.

2 bunches asparagus spears, trimmed
2 avocados
finely grated zest and juice of I lemon
200g smoked salmon
I cup washed mesclun (baby
  salad leaves)
salt and freshly ground black pepper
4 tblsp lemon-infused olive oil
4 tblsp salmon caviar
lemon wedges to serve

1 Cook asparagus in boiling, salted water for 1–2 minutes or until just tender and still bright green. Drain and plunge into ice-cold water to cool.
2 Peel avocados, remove stones and slice flesh. Squeeze lemon juice over avocado to prevent it from turning brown.
3 Layer asparagus and avocado with smoked salmon and salad leaves. Season with salt and pepper to taste. Drizzle with lemon-infused oil and top with salmon caviar and lemon zest. Serve lemon wedges on the side.

SERVES 4

PROSCIUTTO WRAPS

RUSTIC PÂTÉ

There is nothing quite like an excellent flavoured, coarse-textured pâté such as this. Spread it onto fresh crusty bread, close your eyes and you'll be transported to a meadow in the French countryside.

500g pork mince

500g pork belly cut into fine dice

5 slices rindless bacon, roughly chopped

4 cloves garlic, peeled and chopped

1 tblsp chopped fresh thyme

1/2 tsp each ground cloves and allspice

2 tsp sea salt

1/2 tsp freshly ground black pepper

1/2 cup well-reduced beef stock
  (sometimes called meat glaze)

1/4 cup brandy

50g butter

4 shallots, finely chopped

225g chicken livers, cleaned

1 egg, lightly beaten

bay leaves

8–10 slices rindless bacon

1 Mix pork mince and diced pork together with bacon, garlic, thyme, spices, salt and pepper, meat glaze and brandy. Place into a bowl, cover and leave to marinate overnight.

2 Next day heat a pan to medium and add butter to melt. Add shallots and cook for 5 minutes without browning. Remove to cool.

3 Place chicken livers into the bowl of a food processor and blend to a chunky paste. Combine egg, chicken liver paste and cold shallots with pork mixture and pack into a 1.5 litre-capacity terrine dish lined with bay leaves and bacon. Wrap bacon end over paste filling and top with a few more bay leaves. Cover with paper and then tightly with foil or a fitting lid.

4 Place terrine into a roasting pan and pour boiling water to come half-way up the sides. Place into an oven preheated to 150°C. Cook for 1 1/4 hours or until juices run clear when a knife is inserted. Remove to cool then refrigerate overnight covered with a weight to press pâté.

MAKES 1 LARGE TERRINE

PROSCIUTTO WRAPS

Delectable prosciutto, thinly sliced and wrapped around limitless morsel possibilities, makes a great snack at any time of the day or tasty nibbles for after-dark drinks.

fruit of choice – for example, fresh
  figs or dates, sliced fresh melon,
    dried figs or pears, water chestnuts
  or caperberries
paper-thin slices of prosciutto

1 Wrap slices of fruit or individual fruits in a slice of prosciutto and secure with a skewer or toothpick.

2 These salty-sweet mouthfuls are extra good topped with a squeeze of lime or a drizzle of good quality balsamic vinegar.

EGGS BENEDICT

Hot pastrami or grilled bacon make interesting substitutes for the traditional sliced ham. This dish is known as Eggs Florentine if blanched spinach is used in place of ham.

Hollandaise sauce:
1/4 cup white wine vinegar
I bay leaf
150g butter
3 egg yolks, at room temperature
2 tsp lemon juice
salt

4 slices ham off the bone
4–8 eggs (1–2 per person)
4 split English muffins or bagels
freshly ground black pepper

1   To make the sauce, in a small saucepan simmer vinegar with bay leaf until reduced by half. Remove bay leaf and set aside vinegar to cool. Heat butter to melt but do not boil, then cool to blood heat.

2   Place egg yolks, lemon juice and 1/2 teaspoon salt into the bowl of a food processor or a mixing bowl. Process or whisk until frothy and pale. With the motor running or while whisking vigorously and continuously, pour on the butter in a thin and steady stream alternately with reduced vinegar. A thick, creamy sauce will form – avoid using the milky whey, which separates out from the butter, as this will thin the sauce. Adjust seasoning with salt if necessary. Use immediately or keep warm.

3   Grill ham until hot, soft poach eggs in a pan of simmering water. Toast muffins or bagels.

4   To assemble, place ham onto toasted muffin, top with well-drained poached eggs, smother with Hollandaise sauce and season with pepper.

SERVES 4

HOT-SMOKED SALMON & ORZO SOUP

Smoking and heat gives salmon a delicate smoky flavour and a totally different texture to cold-smoked salmon, which is the type most often purchased in thin slippery slices.

4 cups fish, vegetable or chicken stock

2 cups water

1 cup orzo (rice-shaped pasta)

200g hot-smoked salmon, broken into small pieces

1/4 cup basil pesto

2 zucchini, trimmed and cut into small dice

salt and freshly ground black pepper

1   Bring stock plus 2 cups water to the boil in a large saucepan. Pour in orzo and cook for 5 minutes until beginning to swell in size.

2   Add salmon, pesto and diced zucchini and simmer for a further 5–10 minutes until soup is thick and pasta is cooked. Season to taste with salt and pepper. Serve immediately.

SERVES 4

SMOKED CHICKEN & CHORIZO SALAD

Smoked chickens, in my opinion, used to have a nasty chemical characteristic. Methods must have changed because these days I find them very succulent and attractively flavoured, plus they are very convenient to use as they are already cooked.

8 baby potatoes

2 smoked chicken breasts, sliced

3 chorizo, thinly sliced

2 cups washed mesclun (baby salad leaves) or rocket

1 fennel bulb, trimmed and finely sliced

1/4 cup extra virgin olive oil

2–3 tblsp sherry or balsamic vinegar

salt and freshly ground black pepper

1/2 cup toasted pinenuts

1   Cook potatoes in boiling salted water until tender, drain, cool and slice.

2   Toss cold potato slices with chicken, chorizo, mesclun and fennel.

3   Blend olive oil with vinegar and season with salt and pepper to form a dressing. Pour this over the salad ingredients. Toss well and serve scattered with pinenuts to decorate.

SERVES 4

BRESAOLA – Northern Italian air-dried beef, served very thinly sliced. Great as an antipasto.

CAVIAR – prized eggs of the sturgeon (fish) that have been salted and packed into tins. Luxury if you can get it!

CHARCUTERIE – covers numerous preparations such as cured meat, sausages and pâtés, based on pork meat or other internal pigs' bits and pieces.

CHORIZO – pungent paprika flavoured spicy Spanish (and Mexican) sausage that has a very coarse, dry texture. Can be eaten raw or cooked.

COPPA – Italian salted, marinated, pressed and dried pork loin. Served in paper thin slices as an antipasto. Substitute more readily available prosciutto if necessary.

MORTADELLA – a flavoured, smoked Italian sausage that is a speciality of Bologna. Some variants are studded with olives or spotted with dots of fat.

PANCETTA – brine-cured pork belly, which is not smoked but air-dried, and forms the equivalent of Italian bacon. Can be eaten raw but is more usually cooked. Substitute prosciutto if necessary.

PARMA HAM – see prosciutto.

PASTRAMI – beef that has been rubbed in a dry-cure crust of crushed black peppercorns and other flavourings then smoked to cook. Pastrami is usually served thinly sliced.

PÂTÉ – in this instance pâté refers to a meat preparation placed into a terrine dish, cooked and served cold. This pâté is called 'terrine' in France.

PROSCIUTTO – salted and air-dried ham of Italy, the most famous being Parma ham or Prosciutto di Parma. Best served raw in extremely thin slices but will become crisp when cooked. Thinly sliced bacon would substitute at a pinch.

SALAMI – well-seasoned, coarse-textured, salt-cured and air-dried meat preparation that needs no further cooking and is generally served thinly sliced.

SALMON CAVIAR – Salmon eggs that are a glistening, soft tangarine colour.

SAUSAGE – a generic term for a mixture of seasoned, minced fresh meats in a tubular casing.

SPECK – a form of Italian smoked pork that contains a higher proportion of fat than other similar preparations. Substitute more readily available prosciutto if necessary.

Here we're talking about dried pulses (peas, beans and lentils) and grains, which are important pantry items. Many classic international dishes are based on these powerful foods of the dry store. They are convenient, healthy and delicious. Often in recipes one can be exchanged for another — simply experiment to taste their different flavours and textures. If a pulse of another size is substituted, be sure to adjust the cooking time accordingly.

Choose pulses that are recently dried as older ones may be past their best. Store in clean airtight containers in a cool, dark place. Be sure to soak pulses in advance, with the exception of lentils and split peas, which cook quickly anyway. Soaking softens pulses and gives a much better end result. Follow packet instructions, but generally the older and drier the pulse is, the longer it needs to be soaked and cooked. Always discard the soaking liquid, and cook in plenty of fresh water. Never salt the cooking water as this will make the pulses tough. Only ever add salt to the finished dish.

Rice in many countries is a staple, the main meal, with everything else being an accompaniment. In other recipes rice is the accompaniment. There are examples of both to be found in this book.

POLENTA WITH GORGONZOLA

Polenta is a fairly plain dish that easily absorbs the sublime blue sharpness of Gorgonzola.

2 cups water

3 cloves garlic, peeled and crushed

3 tblsp olive oil

I tsp salt

1/2 cup instant polenta

100g Gorgonzola, cubed

1   Bring water to the boil, add garlic, oil and salt. Rain in polenta and simmer, stirring constantly for 5 minutes to cook. Stir in Gorgonzola.

2   Serve like mashed potatoes as a savoury porridge to accompany meat or vegetable dishes.

SERVES 4

RISOTTO OF MEATBALLS & TOMATO

Risotto is one of those singularly satisfying dishes that leaves you wondering what you ever ate before you discovered it!

Meatballs:

500g beef mince

I egg

I small red onion, peeled and
 finely diced

I tblsp chopped oregano

salt and freshly ground black
 pepper to taste

1   Blend all ingredients together and form into 20 meatballs with moist hands to avoid sticking.

2   Pan fry meatballs in a little oil to brown on all sides. Drain on paper towels.

Risotto:

3 cups beef stock

400ml can chopped tomatoes

2 tblsp olive oil

2 cloves garlic, crushed

I onion, peeled and finely diced

1 1/2 cups risotto rice

1/2 cup freshly grated Parmesan

2 tblsp chopped fresh parsley

salt and freshly ground black pepper

1   Heat stock, tomatoes and their juice together in a saucepan.

2   Heat a large heavy-based pan, add oil, garlic and onion and cook gently for 5 minutes. Add rice and stir for 2 minutes to toast but not brown. Add one ladleful of hot stock and stir well. When all the liquid has been absorbed, add another ladleful.

3   Continue to stir and keep adding hot liquid until it is all absorbed. After 15–20 minutes the rice should be al dente (just tender to the bite) and creamy.

4   Stir in Parmesan, parsley, prepared meatballs and salt and pepper to taste. Cover and leave for 5 minutes to steam heat through.

SERVES 4–6

PERUVIAN RICE

This is a remarkable recipe; its preparation, flavour and colouring are altogether striking.

**1/2 cup coriander leaves,
 tightly packed**

**1 cup spinach leaves, stems
 removed, tightly packed**

1 1/2 cups vegetable or chicken stock

1 cup milk

1 tsp salt

2 tblsp olive oil

50g butter

1 1/2 cups long-grain rice

1/2 onion, finely grated

1 clove garlic, crushed

freshly ground black pepper

freshly grated nutmeg

1 Place the coriander, spinach and stock in a blender and blend to purée. Add milk and salt and blend to combine.

2 Heat a large saucepan with a good fitting lid, add olive oil and butter to melt. Add rice and cook for 3–4 minutes stirring constantly; do not allow to brown. Add onion and garlic and cook for 1 minute stirring constantly.

3 Add the contents of the blender, stir well and bring to the boil. Cover the saucepan and simmer very gently for 20 minutes.

4 Remove from the heat and gently stir in pepper and nutmeg. Cover and leave to steam for 5 minutes. Serve hot.

SERVES 6–8

CHICKEN PAELLA

The rice is the most important ingredient in paella. Look for Calasparra, which gives an authentic consistency to the finished dish.

600g chicken thigh meat, cubed

3 tblsp olive oil

3 1/2 cups chicken stock

1/2 tsp saffron threads

1 red onion, peeled and diced

3 cloves garlic, peeled and crushed

2 cups paella rice

2 tsp sweet smoked Spanish paprika

1 cup white wine

3 tomatoes, peeled and chopped

salt and freshly ground black pepper

**3 tblsp chopped fresh marjoram
 or parsley**

1 Heat a large frying pan and brown chicken cubes in a little oil. Remove to one side.

2 Heat stock in a small saucepan and add saffron to dissolve.

3 Add onion and garlic and a little more oil to the first pan and cook until softened without browning. Add rice and stir to heat through and coat with oil.

4 Add paprika, white wine, tomatoes and hot saffron stock to the rice. Season with salt and pepper and bring to the boil, then simmer gently for 15–20 minutes uncovered.

5 Add cooked chicken and marjoram or parsley to the rice; cover to gently steam and heat through for 5 minutes. The rice should be cooked and the liquid evaporated. Adjust seasoning if necessary and fluff up rice to serve.

SERVES 6

GAZPACHO WITH BULGAR WHEAT

Traditionally, bread soaked in water is used to thicken this refreshing cold soup of Spain. While not authentic, I find soaked bulgar wheat gives a pleasant nuttiness to Gazpacho.

1/3 cup coarse bulgar wheat

2 cloves garlic, peeled

6 large ripe tomatoes, peeled
  and de-seeded

1/2 telegraph cucumber, peeled,
  de-seeded and roughly chopped

I red pepper, seeds removed,
  roughly chopped

I red onion, peeled and chopped

I tsp sugar

3 tblsp sherry vinegar

4 tblsp olive oil

I tsp sweet smoked Spanish paprika

salt and freshly ground black pepper

ice cubes to serve

1. Place bulgar wheat into a bowl and pour over boiling water to just cover. Set aside to soften and cool.
2. Blend cold bulgar wheat and liquid with remaining ingredients in a food processor. Purée in batches if necessary, adding extra water to thin if required. Adjust seasoning at end of processing, adding extra salt, pepper, vinegar, oil or paprika to taste.
3. Cover and refrigerate until cold, or overnight preferably to allow flavours to develop. When ready to serve, place a few ice cubes into each bowl and pour on Gazpacho.

SERVES 4

COUSCOUS & SWEETCORN SALAD

Giant couscous is sometimes labelled Israeli couscous, but there are other versions such as king couscous or Lebanese couscous. Novel giant couscous is fun if you can get it, however ordinary couscous is also perfectly fine in this simple salad.

I 1/2 cups giant couscous or I cup
  instant standard couscous

2 cobs sweetcorn, cooked

4 spring onions, chopped

2 cloves garlic, finely chopped

2 tblsp chopped fresh mint

salt and freshly ground black pepper

juice of 2 lemons

1/4 cup extra virgin olive oil

1. Cook giant couscous in boiling water for 8–10 minutes until tender. Drain well and set aside to cool. Or for ordinary instant couscous, place couscous into a bowl and cover with an equal quantity of boiling water or stock. Cover and leave to swell, then fluff up grains with a fork.
2. Remove kernels of corn from the cobs with a sharp knife. Combine prepared couscous with corn, spring onions, garlic and mint. Season with salt and pepper to taste. Sprinkle with lemon juice and olive oil and toss well.

SERVES 4

LENTIL & SPICY TUNA SALAD

This well-flavoured salad can be thrown together with comforting ease.

1 1/2 cups Puy green lentils

3 stalks celery, finely sliced

2 spring onions, finely sliced

1 red onion, finely diced

1 cup drained and flaked canned tuna

2 tblsp chopped fresh coriander

Dressing:

1 tblsp quality curry powder

3 cloves garlic, crushed

juice of 3 lemons

1/4 –1/2 cup extra virgin olive oil

salt and freshly ground black pepper

1 Place lentils into a saucepan and cover with plenty of cold water. Bring to the boil, then simmer for 20 minutes or until tender. If not using Puy lentils, please note that ordinary brown or green lentils will take up to 40 minutes to cook. Drain well and set aside to cool.

2 Mix cold lentils with remaining salad ingredients.

3 Heat a small frying pan and dry fry curry powder briefly to enhance spice flavours. Blend toasted curry powder with remaining dressing ingredients and pour over salad. Toss well and serve.

SERVES 4

BARLEY, PUMPKIN & FETA SALAD

Barley will always be a favourite foodstuff of mine — this must have something to do with the heart-warming soups my mother makes.

1/2 medium crown pumpkin,
  peeled and cut into large cubes

4 cloves garlic, crushed

olive oil to roast

1 cup pearl barley

2 bay leaves

3–4 tblsp sherry or red wine vinegar

1/4 cup extra virgin olive oil

salt and freshly ground black pepper

4 tblsp chopped fresh basil

150g crumbled feta

1 Preheat oven to 190°C. Toss pumpkin cubes in crushed garlic and a little oil and place into a roasting pan. Roast for 40 minutes or until tender and lightly caramelised. Remove to cool.

2 Meanwhile, place barley and bay leaves into a large saucepan. Cover with cold water and bring to the boil, then simmer for 40–45 minutes or until barley is tender. Drain well, discard bay leaves and set aside to cool.

3 Toss cold pumpkin and barley together with vinegar and oil. Season with salt and pepper to taste and serve scattered with basil and feta.

SERVES 6

SPELT & BEAN SOUP

Oval grains of spelt have a distinct nutty flavour and contribute to thickening this robust soup.

3 tblsp olive oil

I large red onion, peeled and
 finely diced

3 cloves garlic, chopped

2 sticks celery, finely diced

2 carrots, peeled and finely diced

1/2 cup borlotti or coco rose beans
 (soaked overnight in cold water)

1/2 cup spelt, rinsed

2 bay leaves

6 cups chicken or vegetable stock

1/4 cup chopped fresh parsley

salt and freshly ground black pepper

1 Heat a large saucepan, add oil and onion and sweat for 5 minutes. Add garlic, celery and carrot and cook over a low heat for 10 minutes.
2 Drain soaking liquid from beans and add beans to saucepan with spelt, bay leaves and stock. Bring to the boil then simmer with the lid half on for 1 hour or until beans and spelt are soft.
3 Purée half the soup and return to saucepan. Add parsley and season with salt and pepper to taste.

SERVES 6

BEETROOT, HERB OR SUN-DRIED TOMATO HUMMUS

Hummus is a little over-exposed and is especially under-whelming if you have suffered the misfortune of a poorly executed bowl of gloop. However, these flavoured variations are pretty exciting.

3 cloves garlic, peeled

I cup well-cooked chickpeas (drained,
 canned chickpeas also work well)

I large beetroot, cooked, peeled
 and chopped or:

1/2 cup firmly packed mixed herbs or:

I cup sun-dried tomatoes,
 roughly chopped

juice of 2 lemons

1/2 tsp chilli powder

sea salt

1/4–1/2 cup extra virgin olive oil

1 To make each hummus, purée garlic, chickpeas and chosen flavouring in a food processor.
2 Add lemon juice, chilli powder and salt to taste. Lastly, with the motor running, drizzle in enough olive oil to form a smooth but firm paste.

MAKES ABOUT 2 CUPS EACH

SPELT & BEAN SOUP

BEETROOT, HERB & SUN-DRIED TOMATO HUMMUS

SEED COOKIES

MOROCCAN CHICKPEA SOUP

Hearty stew-like soups such as this are a meal in themselves.

1 cup chickpeas, soaked overnight in cold water
1 onion, chopped
2 cloves garlic, chopped
1/4 cup olive oil
3 tblsp grated fresh ginger
1/2 tsp saffron threads
1 tblsp sugar
800g canned tomatoes, chopped
1/2 cup Puy green lentils
4 cups chicken stock
3 chicken breasts
1/3 cup long-grain rice
juice of 1 lemon
salt and fresh ground black pepper
1/2 cup chopped fresh coriander

1 Drain chickpeas, place in a saucepan and cover with fresh cold water. Simmer for 50 minutes or until tender. Drain and reserve.
2 In a large saucepan, soften onion and garlic in olive oil. Add ginger, saffron, sugar, tomatoes, lentils and stock. Bring to the boil then simmer for 20 minutes.
3 Add whole chicken breasts, rice and chickpeas and simmer for 15 minutes until cooked through. Remove chicken, slice and return to the saucepan.
4 Stir in the lemon juice and season to taste with salt and pepper. Add fresh coriander just before serving.

SERVES 6

SEED COOKIES

Nibble on these pretty lace cookies to release the aromatic flavours of the embedded seeds.

75g butter
1/2 cup sugar
3 tblsp golden syrup
1/2 cup plain flour
3 tblsp sesame seeds
2 tblsp poppy seeds
1 tblsp anise seeds

1 Place butter, sugar and golden syrup into a saucepan to melt and for sugar to dissolve. Stir in flour and all the seeds then remove from heat. Set aside to cool to room temperature.
2 Heat oven to 160°C and cover an oven tray with non-stick baking paper.
3 Place teaspoonful lots onto prepared paper, spacing well to allow for cookies to spread.
4 Bake for 12 minutes or until darkened in colour. Remove to a wire rack to harden into crisp cookies. Store in an airtight container.

MAKES 20

CHOCOLATE RISOTTO

Okay, you might think a sweet risotto sounds a bit dodgy; well, think of it as rice pudding for hedonists. There, that sounds better, doesn't it?

600ml milk
2 tblsp sugar
2 tsp quality cocoa powder
50g butter
1/2 cup risotto rice
1/4 cup toasted slivered almonds
1/4 cup chopped candied fruit or raisins
100g grated dark chocolate
1 tblsp brandy or coffee liqueur
extra grated chocolate to decorate

1 Heat milk, sugar and cocoa together in a saucepan, stirring until sugar and cocoa dissolve.
2 Melt butter in a large heavy-based saucepan, add risotto rice and stir over heat for 1 minute. Add hot milk and stir to combine. Bring to the boil then cover and gently simmer for 20 minutes until milk has been mostly absorbed.
3 Turn off heat and leave to stand for 5 minutes. Quickly mix in almonds, candied fruit, chocolate and liqueur. Serve hot or chilled, decorated with extra grated chocolate.

SERVES 6

CHOCOLATE POLENTA PUDDINGS

Hot chocolate sponge puds are guaranteed to send eaters into ecstasy and a little polenta adds a crunchy element of surprise.

sugar for sprinkling
250g bittersweet chocolate, chopped
60g butter
1/2 cup milk
1/4 cup instant polenta
1 tsp vanilla extract
3 egg yolks
4 egg whites
1/4 cup caster sugar

1 Preheat oven to 190°C. Grease 6 180ml capacity ramekins and sprinkle with a little sugar.
2 Carefully melt chocolate in a large bowl over a double boiler or in the microwave.
3 Melt butter in a small saucepan then stir in milk and polenta and simmer for 5 minutes. Pour this mixture onto melted chocolate and stir to combine. Stir in vanilla and egg yolks one at a time.
4 In a clean bowl whisk egg whites to foamy soft peaks. Gradually whisk in sugar to incorporate. Fold egg whites into polenta mixture.
5 Pour mixture into ramekins to fill to three-quarters. Place ramekins into an oven pan and fill with warm water to come half-way up the sides of the ramekins. Bake for 20 minutes or until a skewer inserted in the centre comes out clean.
6 Turn out and serve warm.

MAKES 6

BORLOTTI BEANS – a type of bean that has a pattern on its surface that resembles writing. The French variety is known as Coco Roses. Dried pinto beans also make a good substitute.

BULGAR WHEAT– also known as bulgur and burghel and can be fine or coarse textured. Made from wheat grains that have been hulled, steamed, cracked and dried. Bulgar is usually prepared by soaking until tender.

CALASPARRA – Spanish short-grain rice used specifically to make authentic Paella.

COUSCOUS – tiny pellets made from semolina. Traditional couscous takes a long time to cook but an instant variety is available in most delis. If the pellets are of a larger size this may be called giant, king, Lebanese or Israeli couscous.

POLENTA – Italian corn meal that is cooked to a porridge-like consistency and eaten soft or set and then sliced, grilled or fried. Polenta can also be used in baking. Traditional polenta needs 45 minutes' cooking to soften but there is an instant variety available that takes only 5 minutes.

PUY LENTILS – quality French green lentils specifically cultivated around Le-Puy-en-Velay. Puy lentils remain slightly crisp when cooked and have a spicy, nutty flavour.

RISOTTO RICE – Italian rice that has the ability to absorb liquid and still hold its shape while letting out starch to form a traditional creamy risotto. Carnaroli, Vialone Nano and Arborio are all types of risotto rice.

SPELT – an ancient variety of wheat, quite unlike modern wheat. Still used as an ingredient in country soups, especially in Provence. Spelt's oval grains have an appearance similar to barley.

WILD RICE – not a true rice but actually an aquatic grass seed with a nutty flavour and chewy texture. Long, black kernels need long cooking time similar to brown rice.

06:PASTA & NOODLES

There's now a huge array of unusual and amusing dried pasta shapes available from delicatessens — more than ever before. Some people will have favourites. I think it's fun to try them all out and use different shapes for different purposes. And I won't go into describing them all, as upon view they reveal their shape. There are no concrete laws — really any shape you fancy can be used as you wish.

As a rule of thumb, however, smooth wet sauces work well with long styles of pasta such as spaghetti, linguine, fettuccine or pappardelle. Short pasta shapes such as penne, cavatelli, fusilli and rigatoni, for example, are easy to eat with chunky sauces where the ingredients are of a similar size to the pasta. These shapes are also good for pasta bakes. Having said that, I've also used spaghetti instead of potatoes in fritatta — so, even rules of thumb can be broken.

As with pasta, the list of noodles from the East is extensive. Some are available fresh, such as udon, soba and egg noodles. Many noodles come dried in packet-form. Delicatessens, which once may have stocked only Continental speciality foods, now carry many exotic Eastern ingredients due to demand because of their huge popularity. If not available in classic delicatessens, check out Asian-style food stores.

Italians favour dried pasta over fresh unless the fresh pasta is home-made. Good dried pasta holds sauces well, especially if it has any ridges, indentations, or is of artisan quality. Cook dried pasta in plenty of boiling salted water, according to the packet instructions (usually 8 – 10 minutes, depending on type and size) until just tender to the bite or 'al dente' as they say in Italian. Taste pieces of pasta regularly to avoid overcooking. There is no need to add oil to the water but it is wise to separate the pieces with an initial stirring.

Fresh pasta is available in fewer shapes than dried pasta — generally sheet form for lasagne or to make parcels such as ravioli, or in strip form such as tagliatelle or pappardelle. With a more yielding texture, fresh pasta is best with delicate sauces and if the sauce is too wet the pasta will soak up the sauce and become soggy. Cook in plenty of boiling, salted water according to packet instructions (usually about 2 – 5 minutes) until pasta is just tender and has lost its raw flour taste. There is no need to add oil to the cooking water, simply give the pasta a gentle stir. Drain well and immediately to prevent the pasta continuing to absorb liquid or it will be gluey.

BROCCOLI & PARMESAN-STUFFED PASTA

BROCCOLI & PARMESAN-STUFFED PASTA

I am particularly fond of orecchiotte (large ear-shaped pasta cups), however there is no reason why this filling can't be used in conchiglione (large pasta shells) or cannelloni (tubes) or folded into ravioli if you so choose.

16 orecchiotte or other large
pasta shapes
200g broccoli florets
2 cloves garlic
1 tblsp chopped fresh oregano
1/2 cup freshly grated Parmesan
salt and freshly ground black pepper
1/4 cup cream
1 tblsp extra virgin olive oil
2 cups quality prepared tomato
pasta sauce
Parmesan shavings and oregano leaves
to garnish

1 Cook the pasta shapes in plenty of just simmering salted water for 10 minutes or until softened but still holding their shape. Drain and transfer to cold water to cool. Drain well before filling.

2 To make stuffing, cook broccoli in boiling salted water for 5 minutes until just tender. Drain well and refresh with cold water to preserve green colour. Chop garlic and oregano in the bowl of a food processor. Add broccoli and process to purée. Add Parmesan, salt and pepper to taste and cream to combine.

3 Lightly oil a large flat ovenproof dish and fill to 1cm with tomato pasta sauce. Spoon stuffing into prepared pasta shapes and place onto tomato sauce.

4 Cover with foil and bake for 20–25 minutes in an oven preheated to 190°C. Garnish with Parmesan shavings and oregano leaves.

SERVES 4 AS A LIGHT MEAL OR STARTER

PASTA BAKED WITH TUNA & TOMATOES

I won't pretend that this dish is even remotely fancy, but it is full of great flavours. It's a cinch to assemble and very pleasing to eat.

250g small pasta shapes, try macaroni,
penne, orecchiotte or fusilli
1 cup canned tuna, drained and flaked
6 small vine-ripened tomatoes,
quartered
1/4 cup basil pesto
1/4 cup capers, drained
2 cups low-fat sour cream
1 egg, lightly beaten
1 cup grated mozzarella or
cheddar cheese

1 Cook pasta in plenty of boiling salted water according to packet instruction or until just tender to the bite. Drain well and toss with tuna, tomatoes, pesto and capers. Place into a lightly oiled deep-sided ovenproof dish.

2 Blend sour cream and egg together and pour evenly over pasta. Scatter with grated cheese and bake in an oven preheated to 190°C for 20–30 minutes or until hot and cheese is golden brown.

SERVES 4

SPINACH & WALNUT STUFFED PASTA WITH CARROT SAUCE

In truth, any stuffing you like can be packed into pasta shapes — this is just one of many possibilities. Sit them prettily in a luscious sauce and stuffed pasta shapes are irresistible.

16 orecchiotte or other large
  pasta shapes
large bunch spinach
2 cloves garlic
1/2 cup chopped fresh walnuts
1 cup ricotta
finely grated zest of 1 lemon
2 eggs, lightly beaten
salt and freshly ground black pepper

1 Cook the pasta shapes in plenty of just simmering salted water for 10 minutes or until softened but still holding their shape. Drain and transfer to cold water to cool. Drain well before filling.

2 Cook spinach in boiling salted water for about 30 seconds. Drain well and refresh with cold water to preserve green colour. Chop garlic in the bowl of a food processor. Add spinach and process to purée. Stir spinach mixture with walnuts, ricotta, lemon zest and eggs to combine. Season with salt and pepper to taste.

3 Lightly oil a large flat ovenproof dish and fill to 1cm with carrot sauce below (or tomato pasta sauce if preferred). Spoon stuffing into prepared pasta shapes and place onto sauce.

4 Cover with foil and bake for 20–25 minutes in an oven preheated to 190°C. Garnish with Parmesan parsley dust (see page 30) and serve immediately.

SERVES 4 AS A LIGHT MEAL

CARROT SAUCE

Use this sauce to surround stuffed pasta shapes or as a simple sauce for spaghetti, for example.

3 carrots, peeled and chopped
2 cloves garlic, peeled
1/4 cup orange juice
1 tsp sweet Spanish smoked paprika
1/4 cup cream
salt and freshly ground black pepper

1 Boil carrots and garlic until tender. Drain well and reserve cooking water.

2 Purée carrots and garlic with orange juice, paprika, cream and salt and pepper to taste. Add just enough cooking water to bring to a pourable sauce consistency.

MAKES 1 1/2 CUPS

PASTA WITH WILD MUSHROOMS

Little packets of exotic dried wild mushrooms are readily available in delicatessens and speciality food stores. Any variety will add a rich earthy flavour to this dish.

40g dried wild mushrooms, such as porcini, mousserons or a mixture
1/4 cup olive oil
1 onion, diced
3 cloves garlic, chopped
500g fresh speciality mushrooms, such as shiitake, oyster or wood ear, sliced
1 tblsp chopped fresh rosemary
1 cup reduced beef stock
salt and freshly ground black pepper
350g pasta shapes such as penne or spirals

1 Soak dried mushrooms covered in warm water for half an hour then drain and reserve liquid.
2 Heat olive oil in a pan and cook onion and garlic over medium heat until soft but not coloured.
3 Add sliced mushrooms and raise the heat. Toss mushrooms to stir-fry. Add rosemary and stock and simmer to reduce by half. Season with salt and pepper to taste.
4 Meanwhile, cook pasta in plenty of boiling salted water according to packet instructions until just tender. Drain well and toss with sauce. Serve immediately.

SERVES 4

ORZO PASTA GREEK SALAD

To me nothing is more evocative of summer than Greek salad. I've taken the liberty of combining these sparkling salty-crisp flavours with some silken textured rice-shaped orzo. The result is haunting.

1 cup orzo
3 cloves garlic, crushed
good pinch of sugar
juice and finely grated zest of 1 lemon
3 tblsp sherry or wine vinegar
1/4–1/2 cup extra virgin olive oil
salt and freshly ground black pepper
1 red onion, peeled and medium diced
4 tomatoes, seeds removed and medium diced
1/2 telegraph cucumber, medium diced
200g crumbled feta
1/2 cup Kalamata olives
1/4 cup fresh basil leaves, torn

1 Cook orzo in plenty of boiling water for 8–10 minutes or until just tender to the bite and without a chalky centre. Drain and set aside to cool.
2 Blend garlic, sugar, lemon juice and zest, sherry or vinegar and olive oil together to form a dressing.
3 Toss orzo, remaining salad ingredients and dressing together and season to taste with salt and pepper.
4 Place onto serving platter and scatter with basil leaves.

SERVES 4

PEA, PIMIENTO & PROSCIUTTO PASTA

Peas are a smart addition to pasta dishes and are often used in bona fide Italian recipes.

1 1/2 cups frozen or fresh peas

3 zucchini, sliced

100g prosciutto, cut in strips

300g small pasta shapes such as fricelli or substitute penne

1 1/2 cups pimiento sauce (below)

1 cup small Ligurian olives

salt and freshly ground black pepper

1 Cook peas in boiling salted water for 3 minutes then drain well. Pan fry zucchini slices in a little oil to brown. Pan fry prosciutto strips briefly until crisp.

2 Meanwhile, cook pasta shapes in plenty of boiling salted water according to packet instructions or until just tender.

3 Drain well and toss with pimiento sauce, hot peas, zucchini, prosciutto and olives. Season to taste with salt and pepper.

SERVES 6

PIMIENTO OR RED PEPPER SAUCE

This vibrant coloured and flavoured sauce is ideal to slosh over pasta of your choice, or to use as a base sauce for other ingredients. Try adding sliced grilled chicken, Italian sausages or a mixture of roast vegetables to this tasty foundation.

1 cup pimientos or roasted red peppers (available in vac-packs or jars)

2 cloves garlic

1/2 cup chicken or vegetable stock

salt and freshly ground black pepper

1 Purée half the pimientos/red peppers and their juice with garlic and chicken stock. Thinly slice the remaining pimientos/red peppers.

2 Place purée and strips together in a saucepan and bring to the boil, adding salt and pepper to taste.

MAKES 1 1/2 CUPS

PASTA WITH CHILLI-SMOKED MUSSEL SAUCE
This sauce is thrilling — it's vigorous, uncomplicated and sensual.

1/4 cup olive oil

3 cloves garlic, finely chopped

10–12 anchovies

1/2 cup white wine

400g can tomatoes, chopped

200g chilli-flavoured smoked mussels

2 tblsp chopped fresh oregano

2 tblsp chopped fresh parsley

1–2 tsp sugar

salt and freshly ground black pepper

300g spaghetti, fettuccine or pappardelle

1 Heat oil in a saucepan and gently fry garlic and anchovies for a few minutes. Add wine and tomatoes and simmer for 5 minutes.
2 Chop and add mussels, herbs, sugar and salt and pepper to taste. Simmer for another 5 minutes.
3 At the same time cook chosen pasta in boiling salted water according to packet instructions or until just tender. Drain and toss in prepared sauce.

SERVES 4

HOKKIEN NOODLE & BEEF STIR-FRY
Lovely thick Hokkien noodles are altogether slippery, springy and mouth-filling. They give a dimension of texture and contrast to many dishes.

400g Hokkien noodles (or substitute
   egg noodles)

400g beef steaks, cut into strips

2–3 tblsp vegetable oil, such as
   sunflower or canola oil

1 bunch spring onions, trimmed and
   cut into lengths

250g green beans,
   trimmed and blanched

small bunch baby spinach or rainbow
   chard, roughly chopped

1/4 cup oyster sauce

1/4 cup Thai sweet chilli sauce

1/4 cup light soy sauce

1/4 cup water

1/2 cup toasted cashew nuts

1 Cook noodles in boiling water for 2–3 minutes or according to packet instructions then drain well.
2 Heat a wok or frying pan and stir-fry beef strips in a little oil to brown. Remove to one side. Add a little more oil and stir-fry spring onions, beans and spinach or chard for a couple of minutes.
3 Add oyster, chilli and soy sauces and water and stir-fry for a couple more minutes. Add noodles and beef, tossing well. Stir-fry to heat through.
4 Serve in bowls scattered with cashew nuts.

SERVES 4

VERMICELLI NOODLE & PEANUT FRITTERS

All of these ingredients are available in Asian food stores or supermarkets with a good Asian deli section.

100g rice vermicelli noodles

400ml can coconut cream

1/2 cup rice flour

1 cup roasted peanuts, finely ground

1/3 cup finely chopped fresh coriander

salt and freshly ground black pepper

3 egg whites

peanut or canola oil for frying

1 Place noodles into a bowl and cover with boiling water. Leave to soften for 5 minutes then drain well and squeeze dry in a clean tea towel. Roughly chop.

2 Whisk together coconut cream, rice flour, ground peanuts and coriander. Stir in prepared noodles. Season with salt and pepper to taste.

3 Whisk egg whites to soft peaks and gently fold into noodle mixture.

4 Heat a non-stick frying pan with a little oil and fry tablespoonsful of mixture in batches. Turn each fritter once to brown on both sides.

5 Drain on paper towels and serve with a dipping sauce such as Thai sweet chilli sauce or soy sauce.

MAKES 20

NOODLE & VEGETABLE RICE PAPER ROLLS

Slick rice paper rolls make a great snack, light meal or finger food.

100g rice-stick noodles

2 tblsp sesame oil

juice of 1 lime or lemon

1 carrot, peeled

1/4 telegraph cucumber

1 red capsicum, seeds removed

1 butter crunch lettuce

12 rice paper rounds

1/4 cup mung bean sprouts

mint sprigs

1 Boil rice-stick noodles for 2 minutes until tender, drain and run under cold water to cool. Drain and toss in sesame oil and lime or lemon juice.

2 Cut carrot, cucumber and capsicum into long thin strips. Tear lettuce into even-sized leaves or pieces.

3 Dip each sheet of rice paper individually into a bowl of cold water to soften, fold in half and lay out on a clean cloth. Place a piece of lettuce, some dressed noodles, slices of each vegetable, a couple of bean sprouts and a sprig of mint onto each. Fold in base and roll up firmly to expose one end of filling only.

4 Serve with chilli, soy or hoisin sauces for dipping.

MAKES 12

UDON OR SOBA NOODLE SOUP WITH TOFU

Japanese udon noodles can be bought fresh or dried; likewise for soba (buckwheat) noodles, which also work well in this soup.

6 cups good quality chicken or
    vegetable stock

2 cloves garlic, sliced

2 tblsp grated fresh ginger

3 tblsp Japanese soy sauce

250g udon or soba noodles

200g tofu, cut into cubes

1 cup sliced button mushrooms

1/2 cup sliced snow peas

3 tblsp roughly torn coriander leaves

2 red chillies, finely sliced

juice of 4 limes

1   Place stock, garlic and ginger into a large saucepan. Bring to the boil then simmer for 10 minutes to allow flavours to infuse.

2   Add soy sauce, noodles, tofu and mushrooms; simmer for 3–5 minutes to cook. Add snow peas, coriander, chillies and lime juice and simmer for 1 minute more.

SERVES 6

CRUNCHY NOODLE, CARROT & CASHEW SALAD

Noodles are a very noble and satisfying food, which have been known to feed mind, body and spirit.

150g packet Crispy Noodles

2 cups washed baby spinach leaves

3 carrots, peeled and coarsely grated

6–8 radishes, finely sliced

2 spring onions, sliced

1/2 cup roasted salted cashew nuts

Dressing:

3 tblsp light soy sauce

3 tblsp sweet chill sauce

juice of 2 lemons

1/4 cup peanut oil

1   Whisk dressing ingredients together.

2   Pour dressing over combined salad ingredients and toss well.

SERVES 4–6

QUICK PASTA SAUCE IDEAS FROM THE DELI

- Use classic basil pesto, which is available in little pottles, and thin down with some cream or stock or pasta cooking water.
- Melt crumbled blue cheese into hot cream or stock for a rich pasta sauce.
- Grill or fry chopped bacon and mix with raw eggs, cream and Parmesan to make a flowing classic 'carbonara' sauce.
- Chopped hard-boiled egg and prosciutto makes a good dressing to toss through cooked pasta.
- Garlic cooked in quality olive oil is simple and delicious and coats pasta beautifully.
- Some excellent quality prepared tomato sauces can be purchased from the delicatessen.
- Try adding some fresh herbs to tapenade or black olive paste, thin with a little pasta cooking water and stir in some Parmesan.
- Green olive paste is great with sage, blend with a little pasta water and olive oil.
- Sun-dried tomatoes, olives, artichoke hearts and capers are all good friends to pasta.

07:OLIVES & CAPERS

THE RANGE OF OLIVE AND CAPER PRODUCTS IS NOW SO EXTENSIVE THAT I FELT THEY DESERVED
A CHAPTER ALL TO THEMSELVES. FOR THOSE WHO MAY NOT REALISE A CAPER IS DIFFERENT TO
A CAPERBERRY, CHECK OUT THE GLOSSARY AT THE END OF THIS CHAPTER. THERE ARE MANY TYPES
OF OLIVES; DIFFERENT MEDITERRANEAN COUNTRIES PRODUCE FAVOURED VARIETIES. I HAVE HAD
TO LIMIT DESCRIPTIONS TO THE TYPES OF OLIVES FEATURED IN THESE RECIPES ALONE.

OLIVES, THE CULTIVATED FRUIT OF THE OLIVE TREE, HAVE AN ANCIENT HISTORY. ORIGINALLY
OLIVES WERE, AND PRESENTLY ARE, HARVESTED FOR THEIR OIL, WHICH IS PRESSED FROM THE
FRUIT. THE FRUIT RIPENS, CHANGING FROM GREEN TO BLACK — GREEN OLIVES ARE GATHERED WHEN
IMMATURE; BLACK OLIVES HAVE RIPENED FULLY BEFORE PROCESSING. RAW OLIVES ARE BITTER AND
INEDIBLE SO THEY MUST BE TREATED AND PRESERVED. OLIVES ARE PICKLED THEN STORED IN BRINE
OR OIL AND SOMETIMES PACKED IN SALT. OLIVE PRODUCTS ARE SOLD IN MANY DIFFERENT FORMS,
FROM PITTED AND STUFFED TO MARINATED OR GROUND INTO A PASTE.

THE CAPER PLANT IS A HARDY SHRUB THAT GROWS WIDELY, MOSTLY IN MEDITERRANEAN REGIONS. THE
BUDS, FLOWERS, SEED PODS AND SOMETIMES LEAF SHOOTS ARE HARVESTED AND PRESERVED FOR USE
IN COOKING. THE CAPER HAS AN ALMOST INDESCRIBABLE, UNIQUE FLAVOUR SOMETIMES COMPARED TO
THAT OF NASTURTIUM.

CHICKEN WITH POTATOES & OLIVES

Many people are surprised that the chicken pieces do not require an initial browning yet turn out melt-in-your-mouth succulent.

4 whole chicken legs (drumstick
  and thigh)
4 waxy potatoes, quartered
2 red onions, thickly sliced
6 whole cloves garlic, peeled
1/2 tsp saffron threads
1/2 cup Kalamata olives, pitted
1/4 cup capers, drained
2 tblsp olive oil
1/4 cup balsamic vinegar
2 tblsp chopped fresh rosemary
2 tblsp brown sugar
I tblsp cornflour dissolved in a
  little water
I 1/2 cups chicken stock
salt and freshly ground black pepper

1 Preheat oven to 180°C.
2 Place chicken legs into an oven pan or large casserole. Scatter over remaining ingredients in the order listed, blending cornflour and water into chicken stock before adding to pan. Season with salt and pepper.
3 Bake uncovered for 45 minutes. Adjust seasoning if necessary before serving.

SERVES 4

SALMON WITH GREEN OLIVE PASTE

Of course black olive paste is equally successful used in this way, as is caper paste for that matter.

600–800g salmon fillet, cut into
  4 portions
1/2 cup green olive paste (or black
  olive paste)
freshly ground black pepper
extra virgin olive oil

1 Place salmon pieces into an oven pan and thinly spread top surface with olive paste. Season with pepper (salt is not necessary because olive paste is already salty) and drizzle with a little oil.
2 Bake at 210°C for 8–10 minutes depending on thickness of salmon.

SERVES 4

SALMON WITH GREEN OLIVE PASTE ON ORZO PASTA GREEK SALAD

OLIVE PASTE SODA BREAD SPIRAL

This is a great recipe for using up all those little jars of paste sitting in your fridge that you've been wondering what to do with.

3 cups self-raising flour, sifted

I tsp baking soda

1/2 tsp salt

2 tblsp chopped fresh basil

I tsp sweet smoked Spanish paprika

1 1/2 cups buttermilk

3/4 cup black olive paste (or sun-dried tomato paste or pesto if preferred)

extra flour to dust

1 Preheat oven to 200°C. Lightly oil an oven tray.
2 Mix sifted flour, baking soda, salt, basil and paprika into a large bowl. Stir in just enough buttermilk to bring mixture together to form a soft dough. Turn dough out onto a lightly floured board. Roll out to 1cm thick and in the shape of a rectangle.
3 Spread surface with olive paste. Roll up from one long side to form a log. Dust with a little flour and transfer to prepared tray.
4 Bake for 20 minutes then reduce temperature to 170°C and bake for a further 10–15 minutes. Serve sliced to expose filling. This bread is best eaten on the day that it is baked.

MAKES 1 LOAF

OLIVE & ROCKET-STUFFED CHICKEN

This chicken skin loosening trick is a good one — simply slip the potent paste in between the skin and the meat and smooth over to enclose. Once you master the knack it is child's play.

2 cloves garlic, peeled

1/2 cup roughly chopped rocket leaves

1/2 cup green olive paste

4 large chicken breasts, trimmed

3 tblsp olive oil

salt and freshly ground black pepper

1 Heat oven to 180°C. Very finely chop garlic and rocket, transfer to a bowl and mix in green olive paste to combine.
2 Loosen the skin of chicken breasts and spoon green olive stuffing under skins. Place chicken into a roasting pan, drizzle with olive oil and season skin with salt and pepper.
3 Roast in a preheated oven for 20 minutes or until chicken tests cooked.

SERVES 4

BLACK OLIVE SOUP

Yes, you are forgiven for thinking this a little weird! In reality you will discover it to be an elegant soup.

6 firm pears, peeled, cored
  and quartered
2 cloves garlic, peeled
4 cups chicken or vegetable stock
1/4 – 1/2 cup black olive paste to taste
salt and freshly ground black pepper
1/4 cup shredded fresh basil leaves

1 In a large saucepan poach pears and garlic cloves in stock until pears are tender. Add quantity of olive paste to personal taste.
2 Purée mixture in a blender or food processor – this may need to be done in 2 batches. Season with salt and pepper to taste – remembering that the olive paste is already salty.
3 Gently reheat soup to serve hot and garnish with shredded basil.

SERVES 4

PERFUMED OLIVE SALAD

The freshness of this salad is unique – the scent of lemon infuses deliciously into the olive flesh and the deep green crunch of parsley.

2 cups large meaty green olives
2 small red onions, peeled and sliced
2 sticks celery, finely sliced
1 cup Italian parsley leaves
finely grated zest and juice of
  1 sweet lemon
1/4 cup lemon-infused olive oil
salt and freshly ground black pepper

1 Pit olives and toss with onions, celery, parsley and lemon zest in a salad bowl.
2 Drizzle over lemon juice and olive oil and season with salt and pepper to taste.

SERVES 4 AS A SIDE SALAD

CAPERBERRY SALAD WITH SALSA VERDE

These salad ingredients are effortless to assemble but the combination is astounding.

250g cherry tomatoes
8 baby potatoes, cooked until tender,
  quartered
200g green beans, trimmed and
  blanched
1 cup caperberries, drained
1/2 cup salsa verde (see page 92)
4 hard-boiled eggs, quartered

1 Combine tomatoes, potatoes, beans and caperberries in a large salad bowl.
2 Toss with salsa verde to dress and garnish with quartered eggs.

SERVES 4

SALSA VERDE

Salsa verde literally means 'green sauce' and is one of the most vivid and alluring of all classic sauces.

3 cloves garlic, peeled

1/2 cup tightly packed parsley leaves

1/4 cup mint leaves

1/4 cup basil leaves

1/4 cup capers, drained

6 anchovy fillets (optional)

juice of one lemon

1/2 cup extra virgin olive oil

salt and freshly ground black pepper

1 Place garlic, herbs, capers and anchovies into the bowl of a food processor and blend until well chopped.

2 Add lemon juice and process until blended. With motor running, slowly pour in the oil until well combined resulting in a vibrant green sauce. Adjust seasoning with salt and pepper to taste.

MAKES 1 CUP

CAPERBERRY PASTRIES

These intense little mouthfuls come complete with their own built-in cocktail sticks.

225g finely grated cheddar cheese

1 1/4 cups plain flour

1 tblsp poppy seeds

pinch salt

pinch cayenne pepper

1/2 cup olive oil

25 large caperberries, dried with
   paper towels

1 Combine cheese, flour, poppy seeds, salt and cayenne in a bowl and make a well in the centre. Pour in olive oil and mix quickly to form a soft dough.

2 Divide dough into even-sized pieces. Mould a piece of dough to cover and enclose each caperberry. Chill for 1 hour.

3 Bake for 20 minutes in an oven preheated to 200°C or until golden brown and firm. Serve warm.

MAKES 25

CAPER RELISH

This is one of those gorgeous jam-like savoury relishes that you just want to eat by the spoonful!

2 tblsp olive oil

1 red onion, finely chopped

1 cup capers, drained

1/2 tsp black pepper

3 tblsp soft brown sugar

1/2 cup balsamic vinegar

1 Heat a pan, add oil and onion and cook gently for about 10 minutes to soften but not colour.

2 Add capers, black pepper, sugar and balsamic vinegar. Bring to the boil then simmer for 5–10 minutes until syrupy. Cool.

3 Serve with cheese, cold meats or savoury pies.

MAKES 1^1/2 CUPS

OLIVES:

ARBEQUINA – small, round, pale-brown high quality Spanish olives that are a Catalonian speciality.

KALAMATA – Greek variety of olive that is large, purplish-black and glossy.

MANZANILLA – variety of green olive that is often purchased pitted and stuffed.

MARINATED OLIVES – both black and green olives can be marinated in olive oil with added flavourings such as garlic, lemon, seeds and spices.

OLIVELLE – these are small sweet meaty olives from Liguria, Italy. Only genuine Ligurian Taggiasca olives may be called Olivelle.

OLIVE PASTE – a purée of either black or green olives, which may be pure or contain extra ingredients such as capers, herbs or anchovies.

OVEN-DRIED OLIVES – these are olives that have literally been partially dried in ovens. They have a wrinkled appearance and concentrated taste and may be found in jars in delicatessens.

CAPERS:

CAPER – the flower bud of the plant. The buds are preserved in salt or brine or pickled in vinegar and used as an ingredient in cooking, or as a condiment or garnish.

CAPERBERRY – the fruit of the caper plant, being a stemmed seed pod. When preserved in salt or brine, caperberries have the same unusual flavour as capers but a crunchy texture due to the seeds they contain.

CAPER FLOWER – a speciality of Calabria. The mature flowers, as opposed to the immature buds, are preserved in olive oil.

CAPER PASTE – a purée of capers, sometimes blended with other ingredients to form a spread.

SALTED CAPERS / SALTED CAPERBERRIES – until recently capers preserved in brine have been most commonly available, but sometimes caper products can now also be found packed in salt. They need to be rinsed and soaked in cold water to remove the excess salt before eating.

A DIZZYING DISPLAY OF OILS AND VINEGARS GRACE THE SHELVES OF DELICATESSENS. NOT ONLY ARE WE SPOILT FOR CHOICE, CHOOSING IN ITSELF CAN BECOME A DIFFICULT DECISION. WHICH BOTTLE HOLDS THE BEST PRODUCT? WELL, THE BEST WAY TO DECIDE IS TO TASTE THE DIFFERENCE AND THEN PURCHASE THE BEST-TASTING EXAMPLE YOU CAN AFFORD FOR YOUR INTENDED PURPOSE. FOR EXAMPLE, A FINE EXTRA VIRGIN OIL IS BEST FOR DRESSINGS, A MORE BASIC PURE OLIVE OIL IS BETTER FOR FRYING. MANY DELIS HOLD IN-STORE TASTINGS TO PROVIDE SUCH AN OPPORTUNITY.

THE TYPE OF OIL OR VINEGAR USED WILL AFFECT THE FLAVOUR OF THE FINISHED RECIPE. FOR EXAMPLE, VINAIGRETTE WILL TAKE ON A NEW DIMENSION IF TARRAGON-INFUSED VINEGAR AND HAZELNUT OIL REPLACE A MIXTURE OF SIMPLE VINEGAR AND OIL. THERE ARE A MILLION POSSIBILITIES FOR PLAYING WITH TASTE AND TEXTURE THROUGH THE USE OF OIL AND VINEGAR, FROM A SIMPLE DRIZZLE OVER COOKED FOODS, TO BLENDED MARINADES THAT TENDERISE AND FLAVOUR FOODS BEFORE THEY ARE COOKED.

AN INFUSED OIL OR VINEGAR IS SIMPLY ONE THAT HAS BEEN MIXED WITH SOME OTHER INGREDIENT SO THAT THE FLAVOUR OF THAT INGREDIENT PERMEATES THE OIL OR VINEGAR. MANY OF THESE INFUSIONS ARE THE HOT NEW ITEMS ON RESTAURANT MENUS AND ARE AVAILABLE IN DELICATESSENS. THE FLAVOURS ARE OFTEN VERY STRONG — TRUFFLE-INFUSED OIL IS A POTENT EXAMPLE — AND ONLY A SMALL AMOUNT MAY BE NEEDED, SO EXPERIMENT A LITTLE FIRST.

CLASSIC VINAIGRETTE

1/2 tsp salt

1/4 tsp freshly ground black pepper

2 tblsp quality wine vinegar

1/2 cup extra virgin olive oil

1 Place salt and freshly ground black pepper into a bowl.
2 Add vinegar, stirring until salt has dissolved.
3 Add olive oil by pouring in a thin and steady stream while whisking vigorously until amalgamated.

MAKES 1/2 CUP

COOK'S NOTES

– A dressing is only as good as the ingredients it is made from. Use the best quality vinegar and extra virgin olive oil that you can afford and that you particularly like the taste of.

– As a guide, use 1 part vinegar to 4 parts oil. These proportions can be varied according to personal taste, the acidity of the vinegar, or the tartness of the food being dressed.

– Modern vinaigrette-style dressings vary from the classic in that they often contain a higher proportion of vinegar and the addition of many new flavours.

– Garlic and mustard are traditional additions and can be included according to taste.

– A pinch of added sugar will bring out the sweetness of dressed salad ingredients such as tomatoes, onions, and even lettuce and cucumber.

– If left to stand oil and vinegar will separate – whisk dressing together again just before serving.

– These recipes are but a few examples – the possibilities are limitless.

VERJUICE & MUSTARD DRESSING

Verjuice is an ancient ingredient. Presently enjoying a renaissance, verjuice is today available in many delicatessens and speciality food stores.

1 tsp wholegrain mustard

1/4 cup verjuice

1/4 cup extra virgin olive oil

1/2 tsp sugar

salt and freshly ground black pepper

1 Blend ingredients together, following the classic method. Season with salt and pepper to taste.

MAKES 1/2 CUP

ASIAN VINAIGRETTE

Toss lightly blanched Asian greens or simple noodles in this aromatic dressing.

3 tblsp soy sauce

3 tblsp rice vinegar

3 tblsp sesame oil

3 tblsp peanut oil

**I chilli, seeds removed,
  finely chopped**

3 tblsp chopped fresh coriander

1 Whisk all ingredients together to form a dressing.

MAKES 3/4 CUP

CITRUS & GARLIC VINAIGRETTE

Citrus vinaigrette will cause any salad combination to sing.

**finely grated zest and juice of I lemon
  or orange or 2 limes**

2 cloves garlic, crushed

**3 tblsp lemon- or orange-infused
  olive oil**

1/4 cup extra virgin olive oil

salt and freshly ground black pepper

1 Whisk all ingredients together and season with salt and pepper to taste.

MAKES 1/2 CUP

SPANISH VINAIGRETTE

Simply drizzle this wonderfully scented dressing over sliced summer tomatoes, creamy white beans or even pan-fried fillets of fish.

**I small red onion, peeled and
  finely diced**

I tsp sweet Spanish smoked paprika

4 tblsp Spanish sherry vinegar

**1/4–1/2 cup Spanish extra virgin
  olive oil**

salt and freshly ground black pepper

1 Whisk all ingredients together using more or less olive oil according to taste. Season with salt and pepper.

MAKES 3/4 CUP

MIDDLE EASTERN DRESSING
This is incredible tossed through a pile of freshly grated carrot.

3 tblsp pomegranate molasses
I tsp toasted sesame seeds
I tsp sumac
I tsp toasted cumin seeds
1/4 cup extra virgin olive oil
salt and freshly ground black pepper

1   Whisk all ingredients together and season with salt and pepper to taste.

MAKES $1/2$ CUP

PISTACHIO & BASIL DRESSING
This viscous dressing of ground nuts is glorious over a new potato salad.

1/4 cup roasted pistachio nuts
2 tblsp chopped fresh basil
3 tblsp white wine vinegar
4 tblsp basil-infused olive oil
1/4 cup extra virgin olive oil
salt and freshly ground black pepper

1   Purée pistachios and basil in a food processor and blend in vinegar and oils. Season with salt and pepper to taste.

MAKES $1/2$ CUP

CREAMY POPPYSEED & LEMON DRESSING
Try this dressing over blanched green vegetables, roasted root vegetables or chargrilled eggplant.

I tblsp poppyseeds
2 tblsp sour cream
finely grated zest and juice of I lemon
1/4 cup walnut oil
salt and freshly ground black pepper

1   Whisk all ingredients together to form a smooth dressing. Season with salt and pepper to taste.

MAKES $1/2$ CUP

BLUE CHEESE DRESSING

Creamy blue cheese dressing is great poured over baby spinach leaves.

1/4 cup crumbled blue cheese

4 tblsp vinegar or verjuice or
   lemon juice

1/4–1/2 cup extra virgin olive oil or
   walnut oil

salt and freshly ground black pepper

1 Purée blue cheese in a food processor then blend in vinegar and oil until a smooth dressing forms. Adjust seasoning with salt and pepper.

MAKES 1/2 CUP

BEETROOT DRESSING

Beetroot makes a wild dressing for pasta, turning it bright pink, but it's possibly more effectively used in subtle fashion to dress such things as braised leeks or roasted peppers.

I small cooked beetroot, peeled
   and chopped

I clove garlic, peeled

I tsp Dijon mustard

1/4 cup red wine vinegar

1/4 cup hazelnut or walnut oil

1/4 cup extra virgin olive oil

salt and freshly ground black pepper

1 Purée beetroot, garlic and mustard in a food processor then blend in vinegar and oils until a smooth dressing forms. Season with salt and pepper to taste.

MAKES 1 CUP

TAPENADE DRESSING

Toss blanched green beans or asparagus in tapenade dressing for good effect.

1/4 cup tapenade or olive paste

2 tblsp chopped fresh parsley

1/4 cup balsamic vinegar

1/4–1/2 cup extra virgin olive oil

salt and freshly ground black pepper

1 Whisk all ingredients together adding enough oil to form a dressing consistency. Season with salt and pepper to taste.

MAKES 3/4 CUP

BASIC MAYONNAISE

3 egg yolks
1/2 tsp salt
1/2 tsp Dijon mustard
2 tblsp white wine vinegar
1/4 cup olive oil
1/2 cup vegetable oil such as sunflower
or canola oil

1 Place yolks, salt, mustard and vinegar into the bowl of a food processor or blend together in a bowl with a whisk or hand-held electric beater. Process or whisk until pale and foamy.

2 With the motor running or while continuously whisking, add oils in a thin and steady stream until combined.

3 Taste and adjust seasoning or add a little extra vinegar if needed.

MAKES 1^1/4 CUPS

COOK'S NOTES

– Straight olive oil is often overpowering to mayonnaise so it is best to use a mild oil as a base or a mix of 1 part olive to 2 parts plain-flavoured oil such as sunflower or canola oil.

– Lemon or lime juice can be used instead of vinegar to give a citrus flavour.

– Before you start, all ingredients should be at room temperature so that they emulsify easily.

– If mayonnaise splits during making, don't fret, but reserve the curdled mixture. Then start again with another yolk in a clean bowl and gradually add the split mixture, whisking constantly.

– Keep mayonnaise away from heat such as hot foods, the sun or the stove-top, as heat will cause it to separate or become greasy.

– If finished mayonnaise is very rich and thick, whisk in a little luke-warm water to thin down to desired consistency.

– Store mayonnaise in the fridge with a covering of plastic wrap pressed onto its surface to prevent a skin forming.

– Mayonnaise lasts about 7–10 days properly stored under refrigeration.

SAFFRON MAYONNAISE

Sunny coloured saffron-scented mayonnaise works well with fish or chicken or as a dip for crudités and crusty bread.

1/2 tsp saffron threads

1–2 tblsp hot water

basic mayonnaise recipe

1 Mix saffron with hot water and leave to dissolve for 20 minutes.

2 Make mayonnaise in the usual way and blend in saffron water at the end.

MAKES $1^1/4$ CUPS

SESAME MAYONNAISE

If you're into such things as tofu burgers, whack a dollop of this mayo onto the burger bun. Sesame mayonnaise also makes a divine dressing for noodles or crisp vegetable salads.

basic mayonnaise recipe (substitute
    peanut oil for olive oil)

2 tblsp soy sauce

1/4 cup toasted sesame seeds

3 tblsp sesame oil

1 Make mayonnaise by the usual method, substituting peanut oil for olive oil.

2 Blend in soy sauce, sesame seeds and sesame oil at the end.

MAKES $1^1/2$ CUPS

WASABI & CORIANDER MAYONNAISE

Try this tangy green mayonnaise with rare seared tuna or even as a dipping sauce for sushi.

1–2 tblsp wasabi

2 tblsp chopped fresh coriander

basic mayonnaise recipe

1 Omit the mustard and combine wasabi and coriander with the egg yolks in the first step of the method so they are well incorporated. Continue in the usual way.

MAKES $1^1/4$ CUPS

WASABI & CORIANDER, SUN-DRIED TOMATO & SAFFRON MAYONNAISE

SUN-DRIED TOMATO MAYONNAISE

This is a very seductive combination of concentrated deep tomato flavour whipped into the perfect mayonnaise.

2 tblsp balsamic vinegar

basic mayonnaise recipe

1/2 cup sun-dried tomato paste

1 Substitute the balsamic vinegar for the wine vinegar in the basic mayonnaise recipe and complete in the usual way.

2 Blend sun-dried tomato paste into mayonnaise until smooth.

MAKES 1^{1}/4 CUPS

TARTARE SAUCE

Tartare sauce was created for seafood — or perhaps it was the other way round!

1/2 cup basic mayonnaise

1/4 cup sour cream

1/4 cup finely diced gherkins

3 tblsp chopped fresh tarragon

splash of Tabasco sauce

1 Whisk all ingredients together to amalgamate.

MAKES 1 CUP

AÏOLI

Aïoli is an ancient French Provençal sauce that basically incorporates a good dose of garlic into mayonnaise. Aïoli is a natural accompaniment to other Provençal foods such as seafood, tuna, tomatoes, beans, peppers and eggs.

6 cloves garlic (at least), crushed

basic mayonnaise recipe

1 Combine the garlic with the egg yolks in the first step of the method so that it is well incorporated. Continue in the usual way.

MAKES 1^{1}/4 CUPS

OLIVE OIL FRUIT LOAF

This is one of those delightfully old-fashioned fruit loaves that is the perfect thing to enjoy with a cup of tea.

225g pitted prunes, chopped
3/4 cup boiling water
1/3 cup olive oil
1/2 cup raw sugar
1/4 cup golden syrup
1 egg
1 1/2 cups self-raising flour, sifted
pinch salt
1 tsp ground cinnamon
1/2 cup sultanas
1/4 cup dried apricots, chopped

1. Cover prunes with boiling water and leave to soften and cool to room temperature.
2. Preheat oven to 180°C. Grease and flour a standard loaf tin.
3. Place prunes and their liquid, oil, sugar, golden syrup and egg into a bowl and beat well until creamy. Fold in flour, salt and cinnamon then sultanas and apricots.
4. Pour into prepared loaf tin and bake for 45 minutes or until a skewer inserted comes out clean. Remove to cool. Slice to serve.

MAKES 1 LOAF

VERJUICE CHERRY JELLIES

And now for something a little more unusual! You must try these jellies as they are an incredibly refreshing way to end a meal.

Sugar syrup:
1/2 cup sugar
3/4 cup water
16 whole fresh cherries (if out of
season substitute preserved cherries)

1. Mix sugar and water together in a small saucepan. Slowly bring to the boil stirring until sugar dissolves. Add cherries and simmer for 1 minute then remove to cool.

Verjuice jelly:
4 leaves gelatine (or 3 tsp powdered
gelatine)
2 cups Cabernet Sauvignon Verjuice
(white verjuice is also fine if necessary
but is obviously a less colourful option)
1/2 cup sugar syrup (above)

1. Place gelatine leaves in a bowl and cover with cold water; leave to soften. Alternatively, sprinkle powdered gelatine over 1/4 cup water to swell then place cup in a bain marie or microwave and gently heat to melt.
2. Bring verjuice and sugar syrup to the boil. Squeeze gelatine leaves to remove excess water then add (or add melted gelatine) and whisk until dissolved.
3. Place 2 cherries into each serving cup or glass and pour on jelly. Refrigerate for at least 4 hours to set.

MAKES 8 SMALL PORTIONS

OLIVE OIL FRUIT LOAF

OIL:

EXTRA VIRGIN – oil that has been extracted from the first cold pressing of the olives. This quality oil retains the taste of its origin. Use virgin olive oils for dressing foods where the flavour of the oil is important.

GROUND NUT OIL – another name for peanut oil, which has advantages for frying in that it can be heated to a very high temperature.

INFUSED OIL – aromatic oils that have been steeped with other flavourings such as an infusion of herbs, lemon or spices.

OLIVE OIL – has various classifications according to its method of processing. See extra virgin.

PURE – pure oils are extracted from a single vegetable species.

SEED OILS – common vegetable oils extracted from seeds include sunflower seed, canola (rape seed), safflower, sesame seed and grape-seed oils. Pumpkin seed oil is interesting but less common.

TRUFFLE OIL – oil infused with the strong scent of truffles is best drizzled straight onto foods rather than being used in cooking.

VEGETABLE OIL – oil that may have been extracted from either the seeds or fruits (nuts) of plants. The label 'vegetable oil' can also be used to indicate a generic mixture of these oils.

VINEGAR AND VERJUICE:

BALSAMIC VINEGAR – a speciality vinegar from Modena, Northern Italy. Grape must is concentrated then aged for years in a succession of wooden barrels, becoming more concentrated with age to form balsamic vinegar. It has a very dark colour and a complex caramel flavour.

INFUSED VINEGAR – vinegar that has been left with some other ingredient so that the flavour of that ingredient permeates the vinegar. Common examples include raspberry, tarragon or garlic-infused vinegar.

SHERRY VINEGAR – made from sweet sherry, this vinegar has a concentrated, full aromatic flavour. Premium sherry vinegar is crafted in Jerez, Spain.

SPICED VINEGAR – commercially produced vinegar that has a spicy taste due to infused spice flavours. Also available from supermarkets.

VERJUICE – the tart unfermented juice of unripe grapes. Verjuice is used in place of wine or vinegar in cooking, being more acidic than wine and less acidic than vinegar. Verjuice can be used in dressings, marinades, sauces, stews and even desserts, for example, fruits poached in verjuice syrup.

WINE VINEGAR – may be red wine, white wine, champagne or sherry vinegar and has a more pronounced taste of wine than commercially produced vinegar.

Flavour additives to be found in the deli range from seeds and dry powders to perfumed liquids. Such flavourings can be incorporated into cooking in a number of different ways from dry spice rubs and dusting powders, to wet marinades, infusions, dressing and sauces, to baking and desserts.

Dried spices can be found as whole seeds (think mustard, cumin, star anise, etc), bark such as cinnamon, vegetables as in paprika, flowers like rose and saffron, seedpods such as vanilla, or any of these pulverised into powders. There are single ground spices such as paprika, sumac, nutmeg, and the list goes on. There are mixed spice blends traditional to different nations, for example, Indian curry powder, Moroccan Ras al Hanout and Egyptian Dukkah, to name but a few. Other dry flavouring possibilities include coffee and tea.

Wet flavourings embrace distillations such as rose or orange blossom water, liquid pulp such as tamarind water, and syrups made by reduction of juice such as pomegranate molasses. All of these should be available in the modern deli or equivalent specialised food store. Of course there are the numerous flavours of Asian cooking and these are only touched on here if appropriate, as really they demand another whole book to themselves.

SUMAC-DUSTED FISH

The lemony zing of sumac is the perfect flavouring to adorn fresh fish.

8 small boneless fillets white-fleshed fish, with skin on
4 tblsp sumac
salt and freshly ground black pepper
olive oil for frying

1 Make sure fillets are clean and free of scales. Cut shallow slits into the skin side of fillets, dust with sumac and season with salt and pepper.
2 Heat a frying pan and cook fish fillets in a little oil until golden brown on both sides and cooked through. Serve 2 fillets per person with pomegranate molasses beetroot salsa (below).

SERVES 4

POMEGRANATE MOLASSES BEETROOT SALSA

The sweetness of beetroot and the intense sharpness of pomegranate molasses counterbalance each other in this vivid salsa.

1 large beetroot
4 tblsp pomegranate molasses
1/4 cup chopped fresh coriander
1 chilli, seeds removed, finely chopped
salt and freshly ground black pepper

1 Cook beetroot whole in boiling water to cover for about 30 minutes or until tender when tested with a knife. Remove to cool. Once cold, peel the beetroot – the skin will simply slip off. Trim and cut into small dice.
2 Mix diced beetroot with remaining ingredients.

MAKES 1 CUP

TAMARIND-GLAZED TUNA

Tamarind has the most wonderful fragrant-sour taste.

2 tblsp canola oil
2 tblsp shredded fresh ginger
3 cloves garlic, sliced
50g palm sugar or honey
3 tblsp Thai fish sauce (nam pla)
1/4 cup tamarind concentrate
1/4 cup water
600g fresh tuna, cut into 4 portions
4 spring onions, sliced
sprigs of fresh coriander

1 Heat oil in a pan and gently cook ginger and garlic for 1 minute. Add palm sugar, fish sauce, tamarind and water. Simmer for 2 minutes to dissolve sugar.
2 Heat a frying pan with a little oil and sear tuna for 1–2 minutes on both sides for medium-rare, depending on thickness of steaks.
3 Serve sauce over tuna. Decorate with spring onions and coriander.

SERVES 4

SUMAC-DUSTED FISH, WITH POMEGRANATE MOLASSES BEETROOT SALSA ON COUSCOUS & SWEETCORN SALAD

DUKKAH BEEF SALAD

DUKKAH

Dukkah is a spice mixture of Egyptian origin. The recipe can vary from place to place and from family to family — this is a combination I have developed and particularly enjoy.

1/4 cup sesame seeds, toasted

1 tblsp cumin seeds, toasted

2 tblsp coriander seeds, toasted

1/4 cup blanched almonds, toasted

2 tsp bittersweet Spanish
 smoked paprika

1 tsp dried thyme, rubbed to a powder

1/2 tsp freshly ground black pepper

1 tsp sea salt

1 Toast seeds and nuts separately and cool completely. Grind together carefully and briefly so that this does not turn into a paste.

2 Stir in smoked paprika, thyme, pepper and salt. Dukkah is best used freshly made but can be stored in an airtight container in the fridge. Serve with bread and extra virgin olive oil.

3 Note: other nuts can be used instead of almonds if preferred. Hazelnuts are more traditional, in fact, but I personally prefer the subtlety of almonds.

MAKES 1/2 CUP

DUKKAH BEEF SALAD

Dukkah was originally designed to be eaten dry as a dip for bread and olive oil but it can be used as a flavouring ingredient to enhance many dishes such as this salad.

650g eye fillet of beef (from the centre
 of the fillet)

olive oil

finely grated zest of 1 orange

1/2 cup freshly squeezed orange juice

1/4 cup orange-infused olive oil

3 cloves garlic, crushed

1 small chilli, minced, or 1 tsp harissa
 (available in good delis)

salt and freshly ground black pepper

6 vine-ripened tomatoes, quartered

2 cups mesclun (mixed baby
 lettuce leaves)

3 tblsp chopped fresh coriander

2–3 tblsp dukkah (above)

1 Season beef and sear in a little oil in a hot ovenproof pan to brown on all sides. Place pan into an oven heated to 220°C and roast for 20–25 minutes to cook to medium rare. Remove from oven and set aside to cool then slice thinly.

2 Prepare dressing by mixing orange zest and juice and oil with garlic and chilli. Season with salt and pepper to taste. Pour half over sliced beef and leave to marinate for at least an hour.

3 Toss tomato wedges, salad leaves and coriander with remaining dressing, add marinated beef and toss well to combine.

4 Sprinkle generously with dukkah and serve with toasted strips of pita bread if desired.

SERVES 4

FRAGRANT ROAST CHICKEN

Salt and pepper are two of the best flavourings available and simple delicious roast chicken will prove this. Other flavourings can be added to ring the changes when desired. Try rubbing spices or fragrant sauces onto the outside of the chicken or tucking them under the skin to flavour the meat.

**1 corn-fed, free-range or
  organic chicken**
small bunch fresh tarragon or basil
1 lemon, cut into quarters
1 cinnamon stick
4 whole cloves garlic
1 tblsp butter or olive oil
**sea salt and freshly ground
  black pepper**
6 slices rindless bacon

1 Heat oven to 190°C. Prepare chicken by rinsing inside and out and drying with paper towels.
2 Place chicken breast-side up in a roasting pan. Stuff fresh herbs, lemon, cinnamon stick and garlic into the cavity and tie chicken legs together with string to hold in flavourings.
3 Rub skin with butter or oil and season with salt and pepper. Arrange bacon slices to protect breast meat from drying out during cooking and to add flavour.
4 Roast for 1 hour or until the juices run clear when a small knife is inserted deep into the thigh meat.

SERVES 6

PAPRIKA-ROASTED PUMPKIN WEDGES

Pumpkin caramelises beautifully when roasted; such sweetness marries well with aromatic smoky paprika.

**1/2 small crown pumpkin,
  seeds removed**
1/4 cup olive oil
3 cloves garlic, crushed
1 tblsp sweet Spanish smoked paprika
salt and freshly ground black pepper

1 Preheat oven to 190°C. Slice pumpkin into thin wedges. I love how the skin roasts and caramelises, but you can peel it if you prefer. Place wedges into a roasting pan.
2 Mix oil and crushed garlic together and drizzle over pumpkin, sprinkle with paprika and toss well to coat evenly. Season with salt and pepper.
3 Roast for 40 minutes or until tender and caramelised.

SERVES 4 AS A VEGETABLE

SUMAC-ROASTED YAMS

A liberal dusting of dry spices enhances this simple vegetable accompaniment.

1kg yams, trimmed

1/4 cup olive oil

3 cloves garlic, peeled

2 tblsp sumac

1/2 tsp chilli powder

salt and freshly ground black pepper

2 tblsp chopped fresh coriander
  or parsley

1 Preheat oven to 190°C. Cut large yams in half or leave whole if small. Place into a roasting pan. Drizzle with oil, crushed garlic, sumac, chilli, salt and pepper and toss well to coat.

2 Roast for 20–30 minutes until yams are tender and slightly caramelised. Sprinkle with coriander or parsley to serve.

SERVES 4–6 AS A VEGETABLE

SPICY FISH & RICE STEW

This light fish dish includes a generous sprinkling of exotic spices that produce gloriously scented flavours. Don't be put off by the long list of ingredients as the method is dead easy.

1/2 cup jasmine rice

4 tblsp olive oil

3 cloves garlic, chopped

1 large red onion, finely diced

1 tsp Spanish sweet smoked paprika

1 tsp ground coriander

1 tsp garam masala

400g canned tomatoes, chopped

2 cups chicken stock

juice of 3 lemons

1 red pepper, seeds and core removed,
  thinly sliced

1 chilli, finely chopped

1 cup sweetcorn kernels, drained
  if canned

600g white fish fillets, cut into
  2cm cubes

1/4 cup chopped fresh coriander

salt and freshly ground black pepper

1 Cook rice in boiling salted water for 10 minutes, drain well and set aside.

2 Heat a large saucepan, add oil, garlic and onion and cook gently to soften. Add spices and cook for 1 minute. Add tomatoes, stock and lemon juice and simmer for 10 minutes.

3 Add red pepper, chilli and sweetcorn and simmer for 5 minutes. Add fish to gently poach for 1 minute.

4 Lastly, gently stir in coriander and cooked rice to heat through. Season with salt and pepper to taste.

SERVES 4

MUSTARD-ROASTED FRUITS

This is like hot, roasted, whole fruit chutney and is heaven in a spoonful when placed next to ham off the bone.

I cup dried figs

I cup mission figs (sometimes called figlets)

I cup dried pear halves

1/2 cup dried apricots

1/2 cup pitted prunes

I tblsp mustard powder

2 tblsp yellow mustard seeds

1/2 tsp salt

I cup brown sugar

1/2 cup white wine vinegar

1 1/2 cups dry white wine

1 Heat oven to 200°C. Place dried fruits in a roasting pan. Sprinkle with mustard powder, seeds, salt and sugar. Pour over vinegar and wine.

2 Roast in oven until fruits caramelise (about 30 minutes), tossing occasionally.

3 Spoon over a glazed ham or use as an accompaniment to Christmas meats, for example.

MAKES 4 CUPS

NORI CHICKEN ROLLS

This is a play on the now ubiquitous sushi nori roll. It is a spiral of rolled chicken breast filled with Japanese tastes of pickled ginger and nori seaweed. Eat these tantalising rolls as you would sushi.

4 skinless chicken breasts

6 sheets nori (sheets of seaweed)

4 roasted capsicums, skin removed

1/4 cup Japanese pickled ginger

8 –12 slices rindless bacon

2 tblsp mirin (sweetened rice wine)

soy sauce and wasabi to serve

1 Heat oven to 200°C. Batter out the chicken breasts into thin, rectangular shapes. Lay 11/2 sheets of nori over each chicken breast to cover with some overhang at one end. Lay 1 roasted capsicum lengthways at one end of each nori sheet (not the end with excess nori) and cover this with a layer of pickled ginger.

2 Roll up, starting at the capsicum end and finishing with a wrap of overhanging nori (like rolling sushi). Wind 2–3 slices bacon around each parcel to secure.

3 Place in an oven pan and drizzle with mirin. Roast for 25 minutes or until cooked through. Slice to serve hot or cold with soy sauce and wasabi on the side to dip.

SERVES 4-6

COFFEE CUP PUDDINGS

This is reminiscent of iced coffee set into an elegant pudding.

2 cups milk

2 tblsp finely ground coffee beans

3 egg yolks

3 tblsp sugar

3 leaves gelatine

  (or 2 tsp gelatine powder)

1/4 cup cream, lightly whipped

1 In a saucepan, scald the milk with the ground coffee. Remove from the heat and leave for 5–10 minutes for flavours to infuse, then strain.

2 Cream the egg yolks with the sugar until pale, then pour on the coffee-flavoured milk. Return to a clean saucepan and cook over a gentle heat, stirring continuously without boiling until custard thickens.

3 Soak gelatine leaves in water to soften then squeeze out excess moisture. Whisk gelatine leaves into hot custard or alternatively sprinkle powdered gelatine over 1/4 cup water to swell then gently heat in a bain marie or microwave to melt and whisk into custard. Set aside to cool.

4 Blend whipped cream into cooled custard and divide mixture between 6 coffee cups. Chill for at least 4 hours to set.

Froth:

1/4 cup espresso or strong coffee

1 tblsp sugar

1/4 cup Kahlua or coffee-flavoured

  liqueur

1/2 cup cream, half whipped

cocoa powder to dust

1 Simmer coffee, sugar and coffee liqueur together to reduce by half. Set aside to cool completely.

2 Gently whisk this cold liquid into the cream to create froth. Do not over-whip.

3 Pour froth over set custards and dust with cocoa powder to serve. Froth will hold for up to 2 hours in the fridge.

SERVES 6

ORANGE BLOSSOM DATE SCROLLS

Dates and orange blossom water are common ingredients in many pastries, baking and preserves of the Middle East.

200g dried dates, pitted and finely diced
25g butter
I tblsp orange blossom water
I cup water

Pastry:
100g butter
I cup plain flour
1/2 cup icing sugar

1 Place dates with butter, orange blossom water and water into a heavy-based saucepan and cook over a low heat for about 20 minutes until a very thick paste is formed. Set aside to cool.

2 Cut butter for pastry into small cubes; rub into flour and icing sugar until crumb-like. Mix in 1 tblsp water and knead to bring together. Rest pastry for 20 minutes. Preheat oven to 190°C.

3 Roll out pastry into an 18 x 36cm rectangle. Spread with the cold date paste leaving an uncovered edge on one long end.

4 Roll up into a long sausage. Cut roll into 1cm thick slices and place these onto a baking tray covered with non-stick baking paper. Pinch ends together to form almond-shaped biscuits.

5 Bake for 20 minutes or until lightly golden. Remove to a wire rack to cool.

MAKES 24

SAFFRON & VERJUICE POACHED PEARS

The resplendent glow of saffron and the tartness of verjuice enhance this elementary dessert.

3 cups verjuice
I cup water
1/2 tsp saffron threads
peeled rind of I lemon
I cup sugar
8 firm pears, peeled whole

1 Place verjuice, water, saffron, lemon peel and sugar into a large saucepan and bring to the boil stirring occasionally until sugar has dissolved.

2 Add pears and cover with a piece of baking paper pressed down onto the liquid so that the pears stay submerged. Poach by gently simmering for 20–30 minutes or until just tender. Remove pears to a serving dish.

3 Reduce liquid to a syrup by boiling rapidly for about 5 minutes; pour over pears to serve.

SERVES 8

HARISSA – a North African fiery paste made from pounded chillies mixed with olive oil and flavoured with herbs and spices.

MIRIN – Japanese sweetened rice wine available from Asian speciality stores, supermarkets and some delicatessens.

ORANGE BLOSSOM WATER – also called orange flower water, it is distilled from the blossom of oranges. Used mainly in Middle Eastern recipes such as pastries and preserves.

POMEGRANATE MOLASSES – reduced pomegranate juice forms this viscous bittersweet syrup common to Middle Eastern cookery. Possible substitutes are tamarind water, or lemon juice mixed with treacle.

ROSE WATER – distilled from rose petals to produce a strongly perfumed water, used as a flavouring. Look for rose water in delis and supermarkets.

SEA SALT – natural salt that retains seawater trace elements, for example, Maldon Sea Salt. Has true 'salty' taste and no bitterness from additives.

SPANISH SMOKED PAPRIKA – Spanish paprika made from ground dried pimientos (a sweet variety of capsicum pepper) that have been smoked over oak to produce a distinctive smoky, spicy flavoured powder. May be classified sweet, bittersweet or hot. I recommend the La Chinata brand.

SAFFRON – saffron is expensive because it is the hand-harvested and dried stigmas from a variety of crocus flower. However, only a small amount is needed to give an aromatic earthy flavour and strong golden colouring to foods.

SUMAC – salty, sour, lemon-tasting spice powder from ground sumac berries. Sumac is a rich crimson colour and can be found in delis and Middle Eastern speciality food stores.

TAMARIND – the sour pulp from seedpods of a tropical plant. Tamarind can be purchased from Asian and speciality food stores in liquid or compressed block forms. The compressed block needs soaking before use. Soak in hot water and work into a paste, strain and discard seeds.

VANILLA BEAN/POD – the vanilla pod gives greater flavour to cooking than vanilla essence or extract, especially if it is split and the seeds are scraped into the dish. It is actually the seed pod of a type of climbing orchid.

WASABI – used in Japanese cookery, wasabi is a fresh, hot-tasting, bright green paste made from a special plant root that is grated. Wasabi paste can be purchased in a tube or mixed from a powdered form.

ONCE AGAIN, WE'RE NOT TALKING ABOUT HOW TO MAKE CONFECTIONERY SUCH AS TURKISH DELIGHT, NOUGAT, CHOCOLATE PRODUCTS, OR WHAT-HAVE-YOU THAT MAY BE FOUND IN DELIS. THESE CAN SIMPLY BE BOUGHT OFF THE SHELF AND EATEN OUT OF THE BOX THEY CAME IN — ALTHOUGH YOU CAN TRANSFER THEM TO A PLATE IF YOU LIKE! THIS CHAPTER IS MORE ABOUT HOW TO INCORPORATE THESE SWEET DELI DELIGHTS INTO COOKING. HAVING SAID THAT, SOME OF THESE RECIPES ARE FOR ITEMS THAT MAY BE FOUND ON THE MENU OF CERTAIN DELICATESSENS THAT DOUBLE AS EATERIES.

HOW TO MAKE VANILLA SUGAR

This is a good trick to know about so that you can always have some vanilla-flavoured sugar on hand when called for in a recipe.

I vanilla pod

I cup sugar (generally white or caster sugar and sometimes icing sugar)

1 There are two ways to create vanilla sugar. One is to place vanilla pods into stored sugar and it will take on the gentle fragrance and taste of vanilla.

2 A second way is to blend together in a food processor roughly chopped vanilla pods and the sugar to be flavoured.
This vanilla sugar needs to be sifted to remove the excess bits of pod but results in a much stronger vanilla flavour, plus the addition of pretty speckles of black vanilla seeds that turn up in dishes in which it is used.

MAKES 1 CUP

HOW TO MAKE A SUGAR SYRUP

Some recipes such as the verjuice cherry jellies (see page 105), specifically state a need for sugar syrup. Sugar syrup can be stored indefinitely in the fridge and can also be used as a basic poaching liquid for fruit.

I cup water

1/2 cup sugar

1 Place water and sugar into a saucepan and bring to the boil, stirring until sugar dissolves. Simmer for a few minutes to form a syrup. Use as recipe directs.

2 Note: sometimes equal quantities of water and sugar are used to form a more dense syrup.

MAKES 1^{1}/2 CUPS

PALM SUGAR SAGO PUDDINGS

These puddings are based on traditional Gula Melaka. Palm sugar is worth hunting for as it has a very special flavour, however it's not a drama if you can't find it and brown sugar makes a passable substitute.

½ cup sago (soaked in cold water overnight)
½ cup palm sugar, flaked
1½ cups water
grated zest of 1 lime
1 cup coconut milk
extra palm sugar, flaked

1 Place palm sugar, water, lime zest and coconut milk into a saucepan and bring to the boil, stirring until sugar dissolves.
2 Add well-drained soaked sago and simmer for 10–15 minutes, stirring regularly until sago becomes transparent and sauce thickens. Pour evenly into 6 ramekins and chill to serve.
3 Decorate with extra flakes of palm sugar if desired.

SERVES 6

BURNT SUGAR CUSTARDS

These are classic French crème brûlée — that is, creamy custard with a burnt-caramelised sugar coating. They are an extremely stylish dessert and are perennially popular.

1 vanilla bean, split in half lengthways
1½ cups cream
1 cup milk
1 egg
4 egg yolks
2 tblsp caster sugar
icing sugar or light demerara sugar to caramelise

1 Scrape out seeds from split vanilla bean, place bean and seeds into a saucepan with cream and milk. Bring just to the boil, then remove from the heat and leave for flavours to infuse for 10 minutes.
2 Preheat oven to 140°C. Whisk egg, yolks and sugar together briefly in a bowl. Strain cream infusion onto egg mixture and stir to combine. Place this mixture into a clean saucepan and cook gently until mixture coats the back of a spoon. Pour into 6 3/4 cup-capacity ovenproof ramekins.
3 Place ramekins into a deep oven pan and fill with hot water to come half-way up the sides of the ramekins. Bake for 30 minutes to set. Remove to cool to room temperature then refrigerate, preferably overnight.
4 When ready to serve, dust surface of custards evenly with a coating of sugar (I find icing sugar works best). Burn sugar under a very hot grill, with a culinary blowtorch, or with a specialised brûlée iron, until caramelised golden and glass-like. Sometimes several dustings and burnings are necessary to achieve this.

SERVES 6

WHITE CHOCOLATE NOUGAT TRUFFLES
Eating these truffles will cause shivers of delight!

1/4 cup cream
30g butter
250g white chocolate, roughly chopped
1/4 cup toasted slivered
  almonds, chopped
1/4 cup chopped nougat
1 tblsp brandy or liqueur of choice
250g white chocolate melts to coat

1 Melt cream, butter and white chocolate together gently in a double boiler or microwave. Add almonds, nougat and liqueur and stir until smooth.
2 Cool to room temperature and stir once more to evenly distribute pieces of nougat and almonds. Cover and refrigerate until set.
3 Roll mixture into walnut-sized balls and place onto a tray; chill again to firm.
4 Carefully melt second measure of white chocolate. Dip truffles into melted chocolate and place onto a tray lined with plastic wrap or non-stick baking paper to set.
5 Keep in a cool place until ready to serve.

MAKES ABOUT 30

WHITE CHOCOLATE CARAMEL CAKE
White chocolate is intensely sweet but somehow avoids being cloying when cooked within this simple cake.

125g butter
100g white chocolate, roughly chopped
1 cup firmly packed brown sugar
3/4 cup water
1 tsp vanilla extract
2 small eggs, lightly beaten
1 cup plain flour
1/3 cup self-raising flour

Caramel frosting:
100g butter, softened
200g icing sugar
2 tblsp golden syrup
2 tblsp lemon juice

1 Preheat oven to 180°C. Grease and line the base of two 10cm or one 20cm spring-form cake tin.
2 Place butter, white chocolate, sugar and water into a large saucepan over medium heat. Stir until chocolate and butter have melted and sugar has dissolved. Set aside to cool to room temperature.
3 Stir in vanilla and eggs, then sifted flours. Pour into prepared cake tin.
4 Bake individual cakes for 40 minutes or large cake for 11/4 hours or until a skewer inserted comes out moist but clean. Cover with foil if necessary during cooking to prevent over-browning.
5 Ice with caramel frosting made by whisking all ingredients together until creamed and fluffy.

MAKES 1–2 CAKES

MAPLE & WHITE CHOCOLATE BERRY CRUMBLE

Crumble-topped puddings are casual and comforting, and yet composed in individual dishes like this they become elegant enough to serve to guests.

3–4 cups fresh berries such as strawberries, raspberries, blackberries
juice of I lemon
4 tblsp maple syrup
100g butter
I cup flour
1/2 cup sugar
1/2 cup rolled oats
1/2 cup desiccated coconut threads
1/2 cup chopped white chocolate
I cup macadamia nuts, chopped

1   Preheat oven to 180°C. Divide berries between 6 individual ovenproof bowls. Drizzle each with a little lemon juice and some maple syrup.

2   Rub butter into flour until crumbly. Stir in sugar, oats, coconut, white chocolate and macadamia nuts. Sprinkle crumble mix over berries. Bake for 15–20 minutes until golden brown.

3   Serve hot, preferably with lashings of whipped cream.

SERVES 6

SILKY CHOCOLATE TART

Dive into this shimmering pool of the darkest chocolate-centred tart you could ever imagine.

Chocolate pastry:
90g butter, softened
1/2 cup caster sugar
I egg yolk
I cup plain flour
2 tblsp cocoa powder

1   To make pastry, gently cream butter, sugar and egg yolk together. Mix in flour and cocoa to form a firm dough. Wrap in plastic wrap and chill for 30 minutes. Roll out dough to 3mm thick and use to line an 11 x 35cm tart shell. Pastry will patch well if necessary. Chill for 1 hour.

2   Preheat oven to 200°C. Line pastry shell with foil or non-stick baking paper and fill with baking beans. Bake blind for 15 minutes to set. Remove baking beans and paper and return pastry to oven to dry out for 3–4 minutes. Reduce oven temperature to 160°C.

Filling:
100g butter
150g quality dark chocolate
I small egg
I egg yolk
2 tblsp caster sugar

1   To make filling, melt butter and chocolate together in a double boiler or microwave until smooth. Whisk egg, yolk and sugar together until thick and pale. Fold egg mixture into melted chocolate until evenly coloured.

2   Pour filling into pastry shell and bake for 15 minutes. Remove and leave at room temperature to set before slicing to serve.

SERVES 8–10

CHOCOLATE MACARONS

My friend Rachel Carley returned from a visit to Paris in complete rapture over this particular sweet confection (she adored Paris too, by the way). We might be familiar with coconut macaroons, but these macarons (as they are called in France) are an altogether different and charming translation.

I cup icing sugar, sifted

I tblsp cocoa powder, sifted

70g ground almonds

2 egg whites

I tblsp caster sugar

I tblsp icing sugar extra

1   Preheat oven to 190°C. Line 2 baking trays with non-stick baking paper. Mix icing sugar, cocoa and ground almonds together and set aside.

2   Whisk egg whites until firm peaks form. Add caster sugar and beat until thick and glossy. Carefully fold in icing sugar/almond mixture a third at a time.

3   Transfer mixture to a piping bag fitted with a 1cm nozzle. Pipe even-sized 3cm flat rounds onto prepared baking paper. Dust with extra icing sugar and set aside for 10 minutes. Bake for 15–20 minutes until puffed and crisp. Remove to a rack to cool.

4   Once cold, join together in pairs with chocolate cream.

Chocolate cream:

100g dark chocolate, roughly chopped

1/4 cup cream

1   Melt chocolate and cream together in a double boiler or microwave. Stir until smooth and set aside to cool to room temperature.

2   Once cold, beat together to form a whipped creamy paste.

MAKES 12 PAIRS

ICING SUGAR, RASPBERRY & COCONUT SLICE

Bright raspberries are indelibly locked into this dense sweet coconut-scented cake and liberally dusted with a storm of icing sugar.

2 cups icing sugar

1/2 cup self-raising flour

I 1/2 cups fine desiccated coconut

8 egg whites, lightly beaten

1/2 tsp coconut essence

175g butter, melted

2 cups raspberries (fresh or frozen)

icing sugar to dust

1   Preheat oven to 180°C. Grease a deep-sided 17 x 27cm slice tin and line with non-stick baking paper.

2   Sift the icing sugar and flour into a large mixing bowl. Stir in the coconut then the egg whites, essence and melted butter.

3   Pour into prepared pan and evenly scatter berries over the mixture.

4   Bake for 35–40 minutes or until a skewer inserted comes out clean. Stand for 5 minutes before turning out onto a wire rack.

5   Once cold, slice into bars and dust with icing sugar to serve.

SERVES 12

TURKISH DELIGHT CUP CAKES

Turkish delight is so thrilling to eat straight from the box that many cooks might bypass the thought of using it as an ingredient. But this proves it can be done, and with distinction.

125g butter

3⁄4 cup sugar

3 eggs

I tsp rose water

1⁄2 cup sour cream

I cup plain flour

I tsp baking powder

12 pieces traditional rose-flavoured Turkish delight

1 Preheat oven to 180°C. Grease and flour a 12-hole standard muffin pan (or 36 mini) or line with individual paper cases.

2 Cream butter and sugar until pale. Beat in eggs, rose water and sour cream.

3 Fold in sifted dry ingredients. Pour into prepared tins and poke a piece of Turkish delight into each (cut Turkish delight to fit mini size).

4 Bake for 25 minutes or 15 minutes for mini size or until a skewer inserted into the cake part (not the Turkish delight part) comes out clean.

MAKES 12 (OR 36 MINI CAKES)

VANILLA WALNUT CRESCENTS

The freshest walnuts possible must be found for these crescents to become transcendental.

I cup fresh walnuts

125g butter, softened

1⁄4 cup caster sugar

I vanilla bean

I 1⁄4 cups plain flour

vanilla-infused icing sugar (see page 122)

1 Grind walnuts in a food processor until they resemble fine crumbs. Remove to one side.

2 Cream butter and sugar in the food processor until pale. Cut vanilla bean in half and scrape out seeds and add to creamed mixture.

3 Blend in ground walnuts and flour to form a dough. Mould tablespoonful pieces of dough into crescents and place onto a greased baking tray.

4 Bake at 170°C for 15–20 minutes until golden. Remove to cool.

5 Toss liberally in vanilla-scented icing sugar to coat.

MAKES 20

BROWN SUGAR & COCONUT LITTLE PAVLOVAS WITH VINCOTTO

BROWN SUGAR & COCONUT LITTLE PAVLOVAS

I personally prefer my pavs to be crisp and meringue-like as opposed to the marshmallow-centred versions.

4 egg whites

1/2 cup caster sugar

3/4 cup loosely packed brown sugar, sifted

1/2 cup desiccated coconut threads

whipped cream

fresh stone fruit such as apricots, peaches or nectarines, sliced

vincotto (see deli terms)

1 Beat egg whites until stiff and dry. Beat in caster sugar until mixture is glossy. Add brown sugar and beat to combine. Fold in coconut threads.

2 Place a sheet of non-stick baking paper onto an oven tray. Shape 12 small nests of mixture onto paper. Bake for 45 minutes in an oven preheated to 140°C. Turn off oven and leave to cool and dry out on the down heat.

3 To serve, top cold pavlovas with whipped cream and fresh fruit and drizzle with vincotto.

MAKES 12 LITTLE PAVLOVAS

MANUKA HONEY & BURNT BUTTER MADELEINES

These chic scallop shell cakes are very oh-la-la!

180g butter

2 small eggs

2 egg whites

1/4 cup caster sugar

1 tsp vanilla extract

3 tblsp manuka honey (or other strong-flavoured honey)

1 cup plain flour

1 cup icing sugar

pinch salt

1 Heat butter in a saucepan to melt. Increase the heat and cook, stirring constantly until milk solids in butter begin to brown and give off a nutty aroma. Strain into a heatproof bowl to remove milk solids. Leave to cool completely but not set.

2 Whisk together eggs, egg whites, caster sugar, vanilla and honey to combine. Sift together flour, icing sugar and salt and fold into egg mixture to form a batter.

3 Fold cooled burnt butter into batter, cover and chill. Leave mixture for 2–24 hours to thicken and firm before cooking.

4 When ready to cook madeleines, preheat oven to 190°C. Spray madeleine shell moulds with oil and place 1 tblsp mixture into each. Bake for 10 minutes until puffed in the centre, firm and golden. Remove to cool on a wire rack. Repeat with remaining batter.

MAKES 24

MANUKA HONEY & BURNT BUTTER MADELEINES

CASTER SUGAR— a white sugar that is finer than granular sugar (known as super fine sugar in the USA).

DEMERARA SUGAR— a light caramel-like flavoured sugar that is made commercially when treacle/molasses is added to white sugar. Raw sugar is a good substitute.

MANUKA HONEY— a speciality honey from New Zealand with a strong and distinctive bittersweet mineral flavour and powerful healing qualities. Substitute any strong-flavoured liquid honey.

MAPLE SYRUP— a thin golden-coloured syrup made from the sap of maple trees.

MUSCOVADO SUGAR— unrefined sugar also made commercially with the addition of molasses but is a darker brown than demerara sugar. Substitute brown sugar if necessary.

NOUGAT— a speciality confection made with whipped egg whites and honey and often with the addition of dried nuts or fruits.

PALM SUGAR— sap from palm trees which is concentrated into block form and must be grated or shaved for use in cooking. Commonly used in Thai cooking, there are light and dark varieties. It is also know as jaggery. Brown sugar makes a good substitute if necessary.

TURKISH DELIGHT— a thick jelly-like sweet served cut into cubes and rolled in icing sugar. Traditionally flavoured with rose water.

VINCOTTO— a rich, dark, syrupy condiment prepared from the must of late-harvest grapes that are cooked over a low flame then aged in oak casks. Look for vincotto in delicatessens and speciality food stores.

PENGUIN BOOKS
Penguin Books (NZ) Ltd,
cnr Airborne and Rosedale Roads,
Albany, Auckland 1310, New Zealand
Penguin Books Ltd, 80 Strand, London,
WC2R 0RL, England
Penguin Putnam Inc, 375 Hudson Street,
New York, NY 10014, United States
Penguin Books Australia Ltd,
250 Camberwell Road,
Camberwell, Victoria 3124, Australia
Penguin Books Canada Ltd,
10 Alcorn Avenue, Toronto,
Ontario, Canada M4V 3B2
Penguin Books (South Africa) (Pty) Ltd,
24 Sturdee Avenue, Rosebank,
Johannesburg 2196, South Africa
Penguin Books India (P) Ltd,
11, Community Centre, Panchsheel Park,
New Delhi 110 017, India
Penguin Books Ltd, Registered Offices:
Harmondsworth, Middlesex, England

First published by Penguin Books (NZ)
Ltd, 2002

1 3 5 7 9 10 8 6 4 2

Copyright © text Julie Le Clerc, 2002
Copyright © photographs Shaun
Cato-Symonds, 2002

The right of Julie Le Clerc to be identified
as the author of this work in terms of
section 96 of the Copyright Act 1994 is
hereby asserted.

Designed and typeset by Athena Sommerfeld
Printed by Condor Production, Hong Kong

ISBN 0 14 301817 5

www.penguin.co.nz